Working with Elderly

Working with Elderly

K.P. SINGH

SHIPRA

Rs. 900; US$ 45

ISBN: 978-81-7541-889-9

First Published in India in 2017

Working with Elderly

Published by:
SHIPRA PUBLICATIONS
LG 18-19, Pankaj Central Market
I.P. Ext., Patparganj, Delhi 110092, India
Tel.: +91 11 2223 5152/6152
E-mail: info@shiprapublication.com
www.shiprapublication.com

Dedicated to
my beloved
amma Smt. Sushila Singh and
dada Late Shri Chandra Pal Singh

Preface

Sociology of aging is the final phase of an individual's life, where an elderly confronts many difficulties with regard to their physical condition, mental health, and support system. The challenges of aging of course require intervention. One of the interventions that can support wellbeing of the aging population is the profession of social work. This book designs the interventions intended to assist the elderly clients in alleviating problems impeding their wellbeing. In doing so, it aims to assess the impact of social work intervention in the care of the aged. I do hope that this work is going to draw attention for several people and institutions especially social workers who are working for the care and welfare of the elderly in India.

A host of individuals contributed and helped me in bringing out my first book. It may not be possible to adequately express the debt that is owed to the many persons, who made this work possible. It is, however a distinct pleasure to record my gratitude and appreciation to those who have contributed to the development of this work.

I miss the presence of my father, who is no longer physically on the scene but who always looked after my happiness. I heartily thank my beloved mother, uncle, and other family members for their dedication for my career, love and who also remained a source of constant encouragement and support. I will remain in debt to them throughout my life.

I am grateful to Prof. Gracious Thomas for his guidance,

encouragement and affection to bring this work. I also extend my gratitude to Dr. Rituparna Bhattacharya for his support academically and bringing out the work in the present form. I express my sincere thank to Virendra Singh Ji, Prashant Singh, and Ajay for their consent support and encouragement.

I thank all those authors whose works I have cited in the thesis and whose ideas have shaped the conceptual frame work of the study considerably. I take the responsibility for any errors or omissions, if there.

Dr. K.P. Singh

Contents

Abbreviations

ADL	Activities of Daily Living
ADO	Additional Development Officer
AIDS	Acquired Immunodeficiency Syndrome
AIR	All India Radio
BDO	Block Development Officer
BKT	Bakshi Ka Talab
BPL	Below Poverty Line
DU	Delhi University
HIV	Human Immunodeficiency Virus
ICSSR	Indian Council of Social Science Research
IGNOU	Indira Gandhi National Open University
IPOP	Integrated Programme for Older Persons
JNU	Jawaharlal Nehru University
KCC	Kisan Credit Card
MIPAA	Madrid International Plan of Action on Ageing
NCOP	National Council for Older Persons
NFHS	National Family Health Survey
NGOs	Non Governmental Organizations
NOAPS	National Old Age Pension Scheme
NPOP	National Policy on Older Persons
NSS	National Sample Survey
NSS	National Service Scheme
OBC	Other Backward Class

PRI	Panchayati Raj Intuitions
PRS	Passenger Reservation System
SC	Schedule Caste
ST	Schedule Tribes
SWI	Social Work Intervention
UN	United Nations
UNFPA	United Nations Population Fund
UP	Uttar Pradesh
UTs	Union Territories
VDO	Village Development Officer
WHO	World Health Organization

Introduction

Change has been understood as a universal characteristic of all societies and all times. As society shifts from simple to complex, change repeatedly takes place in all walks of social life. We are not able to see all changes in the society because of its slow nature but it happens all the times. Social change is the situation where change takes place in social structure because of failure of transmission of culture, change in external conditions and the strain for consistency. There are various factors, which are responsible for social change such as biological conditions, demographic conditions, technological advancement, cultural conditions, psychological factors, economic conditions, industrialization and modernization, etc. Now, in this fast changing social scenario, every individual face some kind of difficulties in the adjustment. Countries in the world are changing, and the family is the major institution undergoing change. As the family changes, so too does its ability to continue to meet traditional roles and responsibilities especially as related to the elderly members of the family.[1] We have observed several discussions and deliberations pertaining to elderly people in present time. The news related to elder abuse has been seen in several newspapers and televisions. The increasing population of elderly is another area of concerns for the policy and decision makers. This concern is not just a

1. Kosberg, J.I. (1992). *Family Care of the Elderly: Social and Cultural Changes*. Sage Publications.

matter of thinking; it is deeply rooted in Indian culture for care of elderly. Though old age is considered a part of the life cycle, certain emerging trends relating to the population of the elderly have been a cause of concern. The subject of changes in the primary institution namely family and their impact on the elderly in modern India has been receiving a great deal of public attention in the present time. Most of the elderly are living in rural area and changes in the socio-cultural milieu have contributed significantly to the marginalization of the elderly people. Joint family system, which acted as a social safety net for the aged, has given way to nuclear family. Value system too is undergoing rapid changes, which do not always favour elderly. Community is losing its grip to act as a means of social control. In response to the present scenario certain questions emerges as to how do the elderly live in this present changing social scenario. What is their situation and living arrangement? What is the status of their physical and mental health? What type of support system elderly are getting from the family members? Moreover, as we know that old age is the final phase of one's life where elderly confronts many difficulties with regard to their physical condition, mental health, and support system. Social work profession supports the well-being of people by intervening at the points where people find difficulties and Social Work Interventions are intended to assist clients in alleviating problems impeding their well-being. To investigate the answers of the above questions, this book explores the living conditions of the aged in the context of the fast changing social scenario and to assess the impact of social work intervention in their care. The schematic design of the chapters is given below:

In Chapter 1, various aspects of the elderly have been discussed. This chapter provides several important aspects pertaining to the elderly and their care. Old aged has been defined followed by elucidation of various concepts of ageing and its demography at global and national level. This chapter also emphasized the need for the aged care and the importance of social work intervention. In addition, different policies and legislations at international and national level formulated to care the aged have been highlighted. Besides, this chapter explains the emerging need of social work intervention in promoting the wellbeing of the elderly.

The Chapter 2 provides a detailed review of the related literature on the elderly. While reviewing the literature, various aspects specifically living arrangements, physical health, mental health, and support system of the elderly have been given more emphasis from social work point of view. The review of the related literature showed a clear gap for the current research study. The second section of the Chapter provides comprehensive information about the research methodology, which was applied to accomplish this research.

The Chapter 3 aimed at presenting the existing situation of the aged in the two villages, that is, *Goila* and *Madwana*, located near the city of Lucknow. It covers a number of aspects such as demographic, socio-economic profile, availability of basic amenities, living arrangements, physical, mental health, and support system.

The Chapter 4 examines the social work intervention and its impact in the care of the aged and Chapter 5 provides an in-depth understanding about the various issues of the rural elderly through six case studies. Each case is unique in its nature and illustrates how the problems of the elderly can be addressed through introducing social work intervention. Consequently in Chapter 6, it has been observed that the social work intervention has a significant role in improving the quality of life and well-being of Indian elderly.

1

Caring for the Elderly Using Social Work Intervention

Family has always been the primary institution in India. The culture of caring for its elderly members (aged parents and grandparents) stems from the rich values of the society. These values have however been changing drastically over the last one decade. The change is obviously due to the sweeping transformation occurring at the basic structure of the Indian society (Help Age India, 2008). These changes have brought diverse issues pertaining to the elderly care. The institution of family has undergone structural changes as well with gradual transformation from the extended/joint to nuclear family. This chapter provides the rationale as to why the elderly care is highly essential in contemporary era; the various legislations and policies available at national and international levels to promote aged care, how and where can social work intervention play a vital role in the care of the aged?

DEFINING THE AGED

Every country comprises of its own aged population. Ageing represents a peculiar phenomenon in human life. Human beings proceed through a predictable course of biological development from infancy to old age and ultimate extinction. In this development, a human being is subjected to a complex variety of influences both internal and external that add up to the process called 'ageing'. The definitions of the aged population, however, are hedging, and vary from country to country. The United Nations uses 60-year to refer to older people. Demographers also use this line, which divides the younger and the older cohorts of a population. In many developed countries, the age of 65 is used as a reference point for older persons as this is often the age at which persons become eligible for old-age social security benefits. In India, old age consists of ages nearing to or surpassing the average life span of human beings. Government of India adopted 'National Policy on Older Persons' in January 1999. The policy defines 'senior citizen' or 'elderly' or 'old age' as a person who is of age 60 years or above. Therefore, there is no exact definition of "old" as this concept has different meanings in different societies. Defining "old" is further challenged by the changing average lifespan of the human beings. There are other definitions of "old" that go beyond chronological age. Old age as a social construct is often associated with a change of social roles and activities, for example, becoming a grandparent or a pensioner. Older persons often define old age as a stage at which functional, mental and physical capacity declines and people are more prone to disease or disabilities (UNFPA Report, 2012). In this research, people who are of 60 years and above are considered as old. Anantharaman (1982) defines ageing in terms of the regularities or events, which occupies significant position of the life span, resulting in difference between younger and older individuals in structure and function. However, ageing as a developmental sequence is not simply a biological one. It is a social process which involves growth and decline as well. The literature on ageing, in general suggests biological or physiological, psychological and sociological approaches that could be utilized for the purpose of defining the concepts of ageing.

BIOLOGICAL AGEING

In biological sense, ageing means changes in structure and function of some organs and systems of the body during the entire life span. According to Handler (1960), "biological ageing is a deterioration of a mature organism resulting from time dependent, essential irreversible changes intrinsic to all members of the species such that, with the passage of time they become increasingly unable to cope with the stresses of the environment, thereby increasing the probability of death". In the field of biological gerontology, Weiss (1966) and Shock (1977) consider ageing as the sum total of changes during an individual's life span, which are common to all members of his species. Some biological gerontologists consider ageing as any time dependent change or a progressive loss of functional capacity after an organism has reached maturity (Rockstein, 1974; Busse & Blazer, 1980). This change, according to them, may be distinct from daily, seasonal and other biological rhythms. Some biological gerontologists often use ageing and senescence interchangeably. Comfort (1964) preferred the term 'senescence' instead of ageing. According to him, "senescence is a change in the behaviour of the organism with age which leads to a decreased power of survival and adjustment". He describes ageing as an increased ability to die, or an increasing loss of vigour, with increasing chronological age. Birren and Zarit (1985) present a comprehensive definition in relation to the adaptive capacity of the individual in the ageing phenomenon. They define biological ageing or senescing "as the process of change in the organism, which over time lowers the probability of survival and reduces the physiological capacity for self-regulation, repair and adaptation to the environment" (Birren & Zarit, 1985). All these definitions pinpoint to the life-limiting phenomenon, or to the probability of dying and to the differentiation of behaviour that may occur concurrently with an increasing probability of dying. Moreover, the definitions also stress the impact of ageing on the adaptive capacity of the individual.

Busse (1969) speaks of 'primary' and 'secondary' ageing with regard to biological ageing. Primary ageing is the result of inherited biological process, which is time dependent and detrimental to the survival of organism. Secondary ageing is caused by the decline of function due to chronic diseases or other damage to the organism. Primary ageing, which refers to biochemical changes that accompany chronological ageing, is considered to some extent to be genetically determined, whereas secondary ageing is primarily the ageing that has been accelerated due to stresses, emotional tension, physical trauma, disease or other insults to the body. Biological age can be regarded as ones position in relation to his potential lifespan (Birren & Renner, 1977). There is no one age when all the physical functions of a given individual begin to show a decline. Deterioration of various parts of the body proceeds at different rates and is generally so slow that it cannot be measured accurately at weekly, monthly or even annual intervals. Except for certain purpose, it is therefore not yet practicable to use physical criteria as the basis for determining whether or not an individual is old. Biological age can be looked as related to chronological age. Chronological age refers to calendar-clock age. Chronological criterion of age takes into consideration the biological process of ageing. However, it does not consider the individual differences in the performance of age-associated functions.

PSYCHOLOGICAL AGEING

Psychological ageing deals with the evolution of adult behaviour over the life span, which includes capacities, skills, feelings, emotions, and behaviour. Psychologists are concerned with the changes in personality and the external behaviour of the ageing person. They deal with the behaviour that is the product of both the biological and social systems (Birren & Zarit, 1985). Birren and Renner (1980) have defined psychological ageing as "the regular behavioural changes that occur in mature, genetically represented organisms living under representative environmental conditions as they advance in chronological age". However, this definition overlooks the persons who deviate from the population norms, in terms of either disease or environmental conditions. Psychological ageing comprises changes in self-regulatory process including cognition and personality (Birren & Zarit, 1985).

Psychological ageing, associated with old age, includes those related to learning, reasoning, recalling, reminiscing, memory, creativity, sense of humour, vocabulary, sensory motor functions, and mental rigidity.

It is therefore a system where maturity is measured in terms of capabilities, adjustment and knowledge. In this sense, psychological age measures the behavioural capacity of the individuals to adapt to changing environmental demands (Birren & Cunningham, 1985). In psychological sense, old age begins when objectively observable cognitive and perceptual changes and subjective feelings of weakness set in. Psychological age gives primary importance to the adaptive capacities, that is, how well an individual adapts to changing environmental pressures or demands in comparison with the average of his group. Since psychological age involves a mental process, psychologists often use mental abilities, such as memory, intelligence, attitude, changing emotional reactions, and behaviour as the base for demarcating agedness.

SOCIAL AGEING

Sociological ageing comes under the purview of changes in social roles, status and habits in relation to one's group or society. According to Tibbitts (1960), sociological ageing is concerned with changes in the circumstances or situations of the individual as a member of the family, the community and society. The changes and events associated with time, include age grading and social attitudes and behaviour of the society towards the individual, completion of parental and work roles, reduced income, restricted activity and mobility, loss of spouse, loss of authority, decrease in social contact, large increments of free time and relative absence of clearly defined social expectations. Social age is to be understood as a system of segregating people into different levels of maturation according to social factors. It refers to social habits and roles of an Individual in relation to the expectation of his group and society (Birren, 1964). According to socio-cultural viewpoint, a person is termed 'aged' when he distances himself from those roles and statuses, which he was performing as an adult or when he is unable to carry out some important social functions (Havighurst, 1961). Thus, social age is based on social positions and roles. For example, the progression through family roles from being single to married and to widowhood, from parenthood through empty nest to grand-parenthood, provides markers for the definition of the individual as young, middle aged, or old.

The above discussion on the perspectives of ageing indicates that ageing corresponds with change in role and status of individuals. Proponents of biological approach associate the change in role performance with the decline in physical health whereas psychologists consider it with the decline in mental health. Sociological or culturalogical approach associates it with the expected norms and values of a particular society. Thus, ageing is a normal developmental process in which biological, psychological, and socio-cultural phenomena interact. This interrelationship of biological, psychological and sociological aspects determines largely the level of individual functioning, adjustment and quality of life at a given point. Hence, there is a need to integrate the different perspectives for a comprehensive understanding of the problem of ageing. The following section engages on the demography of the ageing population taking into account both the global and the national scenarios.

DEMOGRAPHY OF AGEING POPULATION

It is well documented that population ageing is a mega trend that is transforming economies and societies around the world. It is a cause for celebration and a major opportunity for all. Older persons are the world's fastest growing population group, amid rapidly changing family structures and the possibility of declining family support systems. Population ageing is not just a concern for the developed world, it is occurring fast in the developing countries too, including in those that also have a large youth population (UNFPA Report, 2012).

Global Scenario

Currently, there are 15 countries with more than 10 million older persons and out of these; seven are from the developing countries. By 2050, 33 countries are expected to have 10 million people aged 60 years or above, including five countries with more than 50 million older people. Out of these 33 countries, 22 are currently classified as developed countries. The population aged 60 or above is growing at a faster rate than the total population in almost all world regions.

Globally, the population aged 80 years or above is growing faster than any younger age group within the older population. The population of centenarians, those aged 100 years or over is also growing fast (*ibid*). Table 1.1 provides some of the available data on global ageing population. It shows life expectancy at any age is expected to increase, and which indicates the rapid pace of population ageing.

Table 1.1: Global Ageing Indicators

Sl.	*Population*	*2012*	*2050**
1.	Number of people aged 60+	809,742,889	2,031,337,100
2.	Number of people aged 80+	114,479,616	402,467,303
3.	Number of people aged 100+	316,600	3,224,400
4.	Percentage of people aged 60+	11.5	21.8
5	Percentage of people aged 80+	1.6	4.3
6.	Sex ratio: number of men aged 60+ per 100 women aged 60+	83.7	86.4

Source: UNDESA, Population Division, 2012.
* The population in 2050 has been projected.

The ageing of the world population is progressive and rapid. It is an unprecedented phenomenon affecting nearly all countries of the world. As long as fertility continues to either fall or remains low, and old-age mortality keeps on declining, the proportion of older people will continue to increase. The numbers are staggering. In the past ten years alone, the number of people aged 60 or above increased by 178 million, equivalent to nearly the entire population of Pakistan, the sixth most populous country in the world. The estimated number of older people in China in 2012 is 180 million. The number of people who turns 60 each year worldwide is nearly 58 million, equivalent to almost two persons every second. In 2012, people aged 60 or above represent almost 11.5 per cent of our total global population of 7 billion. By 2050, the proportion is projected to be nearly double, that is, 22 per cent. By

2050, it is expected that for the first time there will be more aged people than children under 15. In 2000, there were already more people aged 60 or above than children under five (*ibid*).

Population ageing is occurring because of declining fertility rates, lower infant mortality and increasing survival at older ages. Total fertility dropped by half from five children per woman in 1950-1955 to 2.5 children in 2010-2015, and it is expected to continue to decline. Life expectancy at birth has risen substantially across the world; it is not just a phenomenon of the developed world. In 2010-2015, life expectancy is 78 years in developed countries and 68 years in developing regions. By 2045-2050, newborns can expect to live to 83 years in developed regions and 74 years in developing regions. While overall the world is ageing, there are differences in the speed of population ageing. It is happening fastest in the developing world. Today, almost two in three people aged 60 or over live in developing countries, and by 2050, nearly four in five will live in the developing world (*ibid*).

National Scenario

Ageing of population is affected due to downward trends in fertility and mortality. Low birth rates coupled with long life expectancies, push the population to an ageing humanity. It is observed that percentage of aged 60 or above is rapidly swelling and even the percentage of persons above the age of 80 is going up over the years. Simultaneously, the ratio of people of "working age" (15-59 years) to those of elderly population is shrinking and even within the working age group, average age is also increasing. For developing countries like India, the ageing population may pose mounting pressures on various socio economic fronts including pension outlays, health care expenditures, fiscal discipline, and savings levels, etc.

By 2026, it is expected that North India population would be younger compared to the South. In India, another paradoxical problem will arise in due course of time. By the year 2026, Kerala will have the highest educated working people with average age floating above the median age of 35 years whereas Uttar Pradesh will have uneducated and less educated working population with average age below 30 years. Although projections indicate that India's population above 60 years will be double in size between 2001 and 2026, the elders will account for 12.17 percent of the overall population in 2026, and being a vast country India may face the problems differently at the rural and urban settings. India will face another problem—despite rapid and consistent economic growth, it will have a huge ageing population who may be far poorer than their counterparts in the West. In India, most of those who have worked in the organised sector get pension and other retirement benefits after attaining the age of superannuation varying between 60 to 65 years. However, much is to be done as at the old age—their medical expenses go up and dependency on children or relative goes up for physical, mental and economic support. Thus in India, though percentage wise graying is not very rapid, but due to its mammoth size planning for the elderly is a huge challenge for the policy makers. The problems faced by the females are more critical compared to that of men due to low literacy rate, customary ownership of property by men and majority of women being not in the labour force during their prime age with only very few in the organised sector. Therefore, the policy for elderly may also keep a realistic achievable gender component. It is to be remembered that sensitising the issue and deliberate public action can dilute some of the adverse consequences of ageing. Educating the mass with high investment in human resource development can overcome these problems to a great extent. To develop requisite policy programmes for the elderly population, there is a need for a study of elderly persons on various aspects and initiate social, economic and health policy debates about ageing in India. However, there is a serious dearth of datasets and analyses to identify the emerging areas of key concern and immediate intervention (Government of India, 2011).

Demographic Transition

The decennial censuses conducted by the Government of India give information on the age break-up of the population, which gives an idea about the trends in the demographic characteristics of the aged. Table 1.2 showed that the elderly population aged 60 years and above accounted for 96 million. While it constituted only 25 million in 1961, it increased to 43 million in 1981 and to 77 million in 2001. The proportion of elderly persons in the population of India rose from 5.63 per cent in 1961 to 6.58 per cent in 1991, 7.5 per cent in 2001 and to 8.2 per cent in 2011 (Census of India, 2011). This is true of other older age cohorts too. The elderly population aged 70 and above which was only 9 million in 1961 rose to 21 million in 1991 and to 29 million in 2001. Besides, the proportion of elderly above 70 in the total population increased from 2.0 per cent in 1961 to 2.9 per cent in 2001.

Table 1.2: Number and Proportion of Elderly by Age Group

Sl.	*Age Group*	*Number (in millions)*					
		1961	*1971*	*1981*	*1991*	*2001*	*2011*
1.	60-70	25	33	43	57	77	96
2.	71-80	9	11	15	21	29	36
3.	Above 80	2	3	4	6	8	9

Source: Census of India, 2011.

The growth rate among different cohorts of elderly such as 60 plus, 70 plus, and 80 plus during the decade 1991-2011 was much higher than the general population growth rate of 2 per cent per annum during the same period. However, Table 1.3 showed that the sex ratio among the elderly in India has favoured males as against the trend prevalent in other parts of the world (Census of India, 2011).

India is one of the few countries in the world where males outnumber females. This phenomenon among the elderly is intriguing because female life expectancy at ages 60 and 70 is slightly higher than that of the males. However, at any given age, contrary to what we would normally expect to, there are more widows than widowers and the reasons for this unusual phenomenon need to be identified. Life expectancy at birth among Indian males had been higher than that of the females until the first half of the 1990s. Apart from this unusual demographic pattern of excess female mortality during infancy and childhood, the phenomenon of age exaggeration among the aged complicates the analysis. Notwithstanding, the several analytical and statistical problems indicated above, the preponderance of females in extreme old ages needs to be brought to the attention of the planners and the policy makers (Government of India, 2011).

Table 1.3: Sex Ratio among the Indian Elderly

Sl.	*Age Group*	*Sex Ratio of Elderly (males per 1000 females)*				
		1971	*1981*	*1991*	*2001*	*2011*
1.	60-70	1066	1042	1075	1028	1034
2.	71-80	1030	1026	1084	991	966
3.	Above 80	950	990	1090	1051	884

Source: Census of India, 2011.

Size and Growth of Elderly Population

In India, as a result of the change in the age composition of the population over time, there has been a progressive increase in both the number and the proportion of aged people. The proportion of the population aged 60 years or more has been increasing consistently over the last century, particularly after 1951. In 1901, the proportion of the population aged 60 or over of India was about 5 per cent, which marginally increased to 5.4 per cent in 1951, and by 2001, this share was found to have risen to about 7.4 per cent. About 75 per cent of persons of age 60 and above reside in rural areas. The size of the elderly population has risen from 12.1 million in 1901 to approximately 77 million in Census 2001. According to official population projections, the number of elderly persons will rise to approximately 140 million by 2021 (*ibid*).

The Trend in the Sex Ratio of Elderly Population

The progressive increase in the proportion of females to males in the elderly population is also evident in the trend in the sex ratio of elderly population aged 60 years or over. The sex ratio among elderly people was as high as 1028 in 1951 but subsequently dropped to about 938 in 1971, again increased to 972 in 2001. Another feature is a relatively higher ratio of females to males in the elderly population than in the general population for all the years since independence (*ibid*).

Life Expectancy at Selected Ages

The expectation of life gives a good idea about the general health status of the people. At a particular age, the expectation of life is the number of years a person is expected to live, on an average, after attaining that particular age. It takes into consideration the morbidity experiences during the whole life cycle of an individual, which depends on the availability of health facilities, nutritional level of the people, etc. With the rapid advancement in medical science and technology, it has now become easier to control various dreaded diseases, which were the cause of high mortality earlier. This has resulted in a steady increase in the expected length of life or life expectancy at birth. Due to various biological factors, women generally live longer than men but still because of some social factors adverse to women, India was one of the few countries of the world where life expectancy at birth was slightly in favour of males until the 1980s. However, because of the improvement in the various socio-economic conditions since then, women's life expectancy in India is now higher than their male counterparts; similar to those observed in many countries of the world. It is also worthwhile to note that in the period 1970-75, average length of life was only 48 years and 59 years in rural and urban areas respectively. Thus, the rural-urban gap in life expectancy is considerably reduced during the last 30 years (*ibid*).

Dependency Ratio

The dependency ratio is an age-population ratio of those typically not in the labour force and those typically in the labour force. It is used to measure the pressure on productive population. As the ratio increases, there may be an increased burden on the productive part of the population to maintain the means of livelihood of the economically dependent (*ibid*). This results in direct impacts on financial expenditures on things like social security, as well as many indirect consequences. The dependency ratio can be decomposed into the child dependency ratio and the aged dependency ratio. In our country, generally, persons aged 15 to 59 years are supposed to form the population of working ages and at age 60, people generally retire or withdraw themselves from work. Thus, in India the old age dependency ratio is defined as the number of persons in the age-group 60 or more per 100 persons in the age-group 15-59 years. The movement of the ratio over time indicates an ever-increasing trend in this ratio, which increased from 10.9 per cent in 1961 to 13.1 per cent in 2001 for the country as a whole. The female old-age dependency ratio as well as the gap between female and male old-age dependency ratio are increasing over time and the two assumed the values 13.8 per cent and 12.5 per cent respectively in 2001, which is a matter of grave concern (*ibid*).

We have observed that demography of ageing population has been increasing rapidly, both at the global and the national level. This growth will result into numerous concerns of population ageing pertaining to their social, economic status, physical, mental health, and support system. Therefore, government, community, family, and social worker will have to pay great attention in the care of aged.

ELDERLY CARE

In recent years, care of the aged has emerged as a great complex problem all over the world and it has become a more complicated problem in India due to variety of historical factors such as changes in Indian culture, family and value system. Care proves to be an extremely ambiguous notion. It means different things to different people. Care means affection, concern, support, and commitment to well-being. It is an art of nurturance. Through care, a person tries to promote the well-being of another. It is enacted in the context of emotional relationships within the complex family dynamics. The ideology of 'love' and 'caring for' should really be the basis of care and respect for older family members (Bali, 2001). Antonucci (1990) delineates three types of informal support to the elderly people. First, emotional support involves the provision of moral and psychological support through sympathetic and caring relationships. Second, is the informal support, which assists the elderly with problem solving and decision making. Finally, instrumental support, which takes the form of help with practical tasks of everyday life. Today, the number of people reaching old age is much greater. Life expectancy has increased dramatically. Increasing numbers of elderly persons means demands being made on the health care systems and on family care. Further, increased longevity implies the need for care being provided over a considerably long period of time. As a result, taking care of the elderly persons not has only become a pressing issue but also a major social concern (Bali, 2001). In the ancient societies, security of the members of the family was very important, for which elders assisted by the young were responsible. Thus, wisdom of the elders and the physical strength of the young combined to guide and continue the family. The older members in the family were then looked after in their old age and also provided nursing care. This was considered as the moral and social responsibility of the members of the family, an expression of gratitude of younger generation towards their elders for what they had done for them in bearing, rearing, educating, training, and protecting them (Chowdhry, 1992). Today, India has highest youth population and in the next few decades, there would be huge elderly population in our country. We have to be ready to face demographic challenges, which will result several issues pertaining to aged care such as health, social, and economic aspects. Elderly care is multi-sided task that has to be shared by the family, community, society, and the state (Bali, 1995). Being a welfare state, Government of India has taken several formal initiatives and started various policies and legislations in the care of the aged. Well-being of the older persons has been mandated in the Constitution of India too. Article 41, Directive Principle of State Policy has directed that the State shall, within the limits of its economic capacity and development, make effective provision for securities, right to public assistance in case of old age. There are other provisions too, which direct the state to improve the quality of life of its citizens. Right to equality has been guaranteed by the Constitution as fundamental rights. This provision applies equally to older persons. Social security has been made the concurrent responsibility of the central and the state governments. The care for aged has been given importance by international bodies as well. The Madrid International Plan of Action on Ageing and the Political Declaration adopted at the Second World Assembly on Ageing in April 2002 mark a turning point in how the world addresses the key challenges of "building a society for all ages" (UNFPA Report, 2012). Many countries including India have adopted various legislations and policies for the well-being of the older people. Let us examine the policies and legislations available for the well-being of the elderly at international and national level.

POLICIES AND LEGISLATIONS FOR ELDERLY CARE

International Scenario

As stated above, the Second World Assembly on Ageing, held in Madrid, Spain in 2002, marked a turning point in international policy debate and action on ageing. For the first time in history, ageing was acknowledged not simply as an issue of social security and welfare, but of overall development and economic policy. The Madrid International Plan of Action on Ageing offers a bold new agenda for handling the issues of ageing in the 21st century. It focuses on three priority areas: older persons and development; advancing health and well-being into old age; and ensuring enabling and supportive environments. Responding to growing concern over the speed and scale of global ageing, the General Assembly of the United Nations adopted the consensus of the Madrid International Plan of Action to guide the Governments, the United Nations and the civil societies to face the challenges and fulfill the enormous potential of population ageing. Indeed, these plans a resource for policymaking, suggesting ways for the Governments, non-governmental organizations, and other actors to reorient the ways in which their societies perceive, interact with and care for their older citizens. In addition, it also represents the first time the governments agreed upon to link the questions of ageing to other frameworks for social and economic development and human rights, most notably those agreed to at the United Nations conferences and summits of the past decade. It stressed the opportunity for older persons to contribute to development, with older persons embraced as a resource, rather than in need of care and support. Its overall objective was to create a 'society for all' in which 'persons everywhere are able to age with security and dignity and to continue to participate in their societies as citizens with full rights' (*ibid*).

Since 2002, it appears that a number of countries now have holistic policies or strategies that allow for ageing concerns to be translated into existing and new laws, policies and programmes. Even though these policies, plans or strategies on older persons are age-specific, their main objective is to mainstream ageing into other policy areas. One of the Madrid Plan's recommendations specifically relates to age-mainstreaming. For this reason, it is important to mainstream older persons into existing legislations, which may not be age-specific but will take forward the Madrid Plan's provisions. Nevertheless, despite the clear recommendation of the Madrid Plan on mainstreaming that there be action to develop a national plan of action on ageing to harmonize the inclusion of ageing into priority policies. Table 1.4 presents the list of the countries who have adopted the national policies on ageing since 2002.

Following the Madrid International Plan of Action on Ageing, these policies, plans and strategies cover a wide range of issues relevant to older persons and population ageing. While this is positive indication of action under the three priority directions, more evidence is needed to demonstrate that provisions are translated into mainstream policymaking. Legal instruments are essential to enable the assigning of

Table 1.4: Countries Adopted National Policies on Ageing Adopted Since 2002

Country	*Name of the Policy*
Ghana	National ageing policy "ageing with security and dignity" and implementation action plan, 2010
Kenya	National policy on older persons and ageing, 2009
Mozambique	National policy on older persons, 2002 and national plan for older people, 2006-2010
South Africa	South Africa older persons' policy, 2006
Uganda	National policy for older persons, 2009
Tanzania	National ageing policy, 2003
Tunisia	Decennial plan to care about the elderly, 2003
Bahrain	National strategy and document for elderly rights
Egypt	National strategy and plan of action, 2007
Jordan	Strategy for the older population "active, healthy ageing and old age care in Jordan", 2008
Occupied Palestinian Territory	National strategic plan to care for the elderly and working plan of the Madrid plan
Oman	National strategy and plan of action, 2007-2008
Qatar	National strategy on ageing, 2007
Saudi Arabia	National strategic plan for healthy ageing, 2010-2015
Syrian Arab Republic	National strategic plan, 2003-2015 and national plan of social and health care for the aged
Australia	Australian local government population ageing action plan, 2004-2009
Bangladesh	National policy on ageing, 2007
Cambodia	Policy for the elderly, 2003
India	National policy on older persons, 1999
Indonesia	National plan of action for older persons, 2008
Leo People's Democratic Republic	National policy on the elderly, 2005
Nepal	National action plan for senior citizens, 2005
Philippines	Philippines plan of action for older persons, 2005
Thailand	2nd national plan for older persons, 2009
Viet Nam	Law on elderly 2010 and action plans, 2005-2010
Albania	The document of cross sector policies on ageing, 2008
Austria	Federal law on the promotion of affairs of the older generation, 2009 (last amendment)
Cyprus	Action plan for older persons, 2005-2015

Country	*Name of the Policy*
Czech	National programme of preparation for ageing for the period, 2003-2007 and 2008-2012
Finland	Finland for all ages, 2004
Germany	Old age creates something new, 2008
Hungary	National strategy on elder affairs, 2009
Liechtenstein	National policy on ageing "future ageing", 2006
Lithuania	National strategy of overcoming the consequences of ageing
Russian Federation	Federal programme older generation, 2002-2010
Serbia	National strategy on ageing, 2006
Sweden	National policy on elderly care
The former Yugoslav Republic of Macedonia	National strategy for the elderly, 2010-020
Turkey	The situation of elderly people in turkey and national plan of action on ageing, 2007
United Kingdom	Cross-government strategy opportunity age, 2005
Belize	National policy of older persons, 2002 and national plan of action for older persons, 2003-2008
Colombia	National policy on ageing, 2007
Guatemala	National programme for older persons, 2005
Panama	National policy in favour of older persons, 2004
Paraguay	Proposal for a national plan of public policies for older persons, 2010
Peru	National plan for older persons, 2006-2010
Trinidad and Tobago	National policy on ageing, 2007
Uruguay	National policy on ageing, 2004

Source: UNFPA Report, 2011.

resources to issues of ageing as laid out in the Madrid Plan. There are examples of legislation specifically referring to older persons (see Table 1.5). In Pakistan (the Senior Citizens Bill) and Sudan (the Older Persons Law), legislation is under discussion but has not yet been approved.

Most of the older persons in the world live in rural areas. While the younger people often migrate to urban dwellings to find jobs, older persons increasingly stay behind stripped off their traditional support

Table 1.5: Countries having National Legislation on Ageing

Country	*Name of the Legislation*
Brazil	Statute of the older person, 2003
India	The maintenance and welfare of parents and senior citizens act, 2007
Madagascar	Law no. 2008/030 protection of older people's rights, 2008
Nepal	Senior citizens act 2007 and senior citizens regulation, 2009
Nicaragua	Law for older persons, 2010
Peru	Law of older persons, 2006
Philippines	Expanded senior citizens act, 2010
South Africa	Older persons act, 2006
Thailand	Older persons act, 2003
Viet Nam	Law on elderly, 2010

Source: UNFPA Report, 2011.

networks. Largely isolated from policy decision makers, they take the full brunt of rapidly changing policies, of environmental disasters, disease, and increasing poverty. The Madrid International Plan of Action on Ageing (MIPAA) adopted by UN Member States in 2002 addresses rural ageing issues in its Priority Direction I: older persons and development. The plan particularly aims at the "improvement of living conditions and infrastructure in rural areas" and the "alleviation of the marginalization of older persons in rural areas." The MIPAA dedicates a section to health issues of older persons and those that care for them. Under Priority direction II: advancing health and well-being into old age, MIPAA lists six main health topics: health promotion and well-being throughout life, universal and equal access to health-care services, older persons and HIV/AIDS, training of care providers and health professionals, as well as mental health needs of older persons and older persons with disabilities. Under Priority direction III: ensuring enabling and supportive environments, MIPAA specifically refers to "care and support for caregivers" that urges provision of care and services for older persons and support for their caregivers, particularly older women (*ibid*).

Therefore, there are several policies and legislations available across the world to provide care and support to the elderly in the world. However, there are still some other countries that do not have specific policies and legislations for the elderly care.

National Scenario

Need of social security policies for the welfare of the elderly in India causes greater concern for two main reasons: the percentage of the aged in the population is rising and the ability of the family to support and take care of the aged is diminishing. Therefore, it has now become imperative for the society to accept greater responsibility to facilitate the social adjustment of the aged. Three main steps the government has taken in connection with the care of the aged. First, the government has enacted legislations to affirm the duty of every person having sufficient means to maintain and look after his aged or infirm parents who are not able to maintain himself or herself. This step of the government only boils down to overseeing the traditional role of the family in providing care and support to the aged. This legislation, however, is of no material use as no parent is willing to go to a court of law to extract support from an unwilling child. The second step, the government has taken is to assume partial responsibility for supporting the destitute aged who does not have earning children or children with sufficient income to support them. The government provides old age pensions to the destitute aged, as well as, gives grants-in-aid to the institutions, which take care of such persons. The old age pensions, however, consist of meager amounts barely adequate for subsistence. The third step, the government has taken in respect of the aged is to pass legislation to ensure retirement benefits, such as, gratuity, pension and provident fund, to be paid by the employers to the aged who are compulsorily retired. Such legislation applies to the larger enterprises and, as such, these benefits are derived by only a small segment of the aged. Besides the government, there are a number of non-governmental organisations (NGOs) which offer various kinds of services to the aged. The services provided by the NGOs include institutional services in the form of old-age homes, vocational services and occupational therapy, non-institutional support systems including medical, psychiatric and rehabilitation services, nutritional care, recreation, counseling, education, training and awareness, and day care centres (Ministry of Social Justice and Empowerment, 2014).

Although this list is impressive, these services are available only in some parts of the country and especially in the big cities. The vast majority of the aged is not covered by any public provision of old-age support whether extended by the Government or the NGOs. In this regard, the Government of India introduced various policies and programmes for the welfare of the elderly to provide self-respect and dignity of an individual.

Legislations

The Maintenance and Welfare of Parents and Senior Citizens Act, 2007 was enacted in December 2007, to ensure need based maintenance for parents and senior citizens and their welfare. General improvement in the health care facilities over the years is one of the main reasons for continuing increase in proportion of population of senior citizens. Ensuring that they not merely live longer, but lead a secure, dignified and productive life is a major challenge.

National Policy on Older Persons (NPOP), 1999

The National Policy on Older Persons (NPOP) was announced in January 1999 to reaffirm the commitment to ensure the well-being of the older persons. The policy envisages State support to ensure financial and food security, health care, shelter and other needs of the older persons, equitable share in development, protection against abuse and exploitation, and availability of services to improve the quality of their lives.

National Council for Older Persons

In pursuance of the NPOP, a National Council for Older Persons (NCOP) was constituted in 1999 under the Chairpersonship of the Minister for Social Justice and Empowerment to oversee implementation of the policy. The NCOP is the highest body to advice the Government in the formulation and implementation of policy and programmes for the aged. The Council was re-constituted in 2005 with members comprising Central and State governments representatives, representatives of NGOs, citizen's groups, retired person's associations, and experts in the field of law, social welfare, and medicine.

Maintenance and Welfare of Parents and Senior Citizens Act, 2007

The Maintenance and Welfare of Parents and Senior Citizens Act, 2007 was enacted in December 2007 to ensure need based maintenance for parents and senior citizens and their welfare. All Union Territories brought the Act into force on 3rd February 2010.

Central Sector Scheme of Integrated Programme for Older Persons (IPOP)

An Integrated Programme for Older Persons (IPOP) is being implemented since 1992 with the objective of improving the quality of life of senior citizens by providing basic amenities like shelter, food, medical care, and entertainment opportunities and by encouraging productive and active ageing through providing support for capacity building of the governments/NGOs, Panchayati Raj Institutions or local bodies and the communities at large. Under the scheme, financial assistance up to 90 per cent of the project cost is provided to non-governmental organizations for establishing and maintaining old age homes, day care centres and mobile Medicare units. The scheme has been made flexible so as to meet the diverse needs of the older persons including reinforcement and strengthening of the family, awareness generation on issues pertaining to older persons, popularization of the concept of lifelong preparation for old age, facilitating productive ageing, etc. The scheme has been revised on 1st April 2008. Besides, increases in amount of financial assistance for existing projects, several other innovative projects have been added as being eligible for assistance under the scheme.

Schemes of other Ministries

Other ministries like Health and Family Welfare, Rural Development, and Railways, etc. are offering facilities for the older people. The Ministry of Health and Family Welfare provides the facilities to senior citizens such as separate queues for older persons in government hospitals, two National Institutes on Ageing at Delhi and Chennai have been set up. Alongside, a Geriatric Departments in 25 medical colleges have also been set up. The Ministry of Rural Development has implemented the National Old-age Pension Scheme (NOAPS) for persons above 60 years belonging to a household below poverty line. Central assistance is given towards pension at Rs. 200 per month, which is meant to be supplemented by at least an equal contribution by the States so that each beneficiary receives a pension of at least Rs. 400 per month. The Ministry of Railways provides the following facilities to senior citizens: separate ticket counters for citizens of aged 60 years and above at various Passenger Reservation System (PRS) centres (if the average demand per shift is more than 120 tickets); 30 per cent and 50 per cent concession in rail fares for male and female senior citizens respectively.

Therefore, the Government of India has initiated several legislations and policies pertaining to the elderly. However, there are still several problems, which elderly face in their daily lives. Ineffective implementation of these policies could not address the main purpose of the rural elderly. Rural elderly needs a holistic and integrated help for their problems as they are not highly literate. The awareness level among the elderly is also not up to the mark with regard to these problems. The major challenge is support system, which is deteriorating day by day largely due to family transition and occupation. Thus, there is a need for such a system that not only solves the problems of elderly but also can understand and maintain their dignity. In the said context, social workers are skilled to understand the human behaviour and solve their problems by maintaining their dignity and worth required by elderly. Therefore, there is a need for social work intervention in the care of the aged. Let us now examine how and where social worker can intervene in the wellbeing of the elderly.

NEED FOR SOCIAL WORK INTERVENTION

The central goal of social work has been to enable people to improve their social functioning; to carry out their social roles in a way that is consistent with their ego capacity. A major focus has been on socially assisting people to cope with life situations and conditions, which present difficulties. Social work has wide range of activities such as social reforms at one end and at the micro level, it helps individual in need. It covers large variety of services as well as policy formulation. Treatment of disturbed relationships among people, the procurement of financial aid through financial assistance or supplementary income, support during crisis and stress situations belong to segment of ameliorative services while on the same continuum. The social work profession has its methods of treatment such as casework (working with individuals), group work (working with groups) and community organisation (helping community to meet its needs through mobilisation of resources). These methods are used according to the needs of the individuals.

Therefore, social work intervention can play a pertinent role in the care of the aged. Older people have significant social, economic and health implications at the individual, family, and societal levels. Population ageing is raising concerns about the ability of the people to provide adequate social protection and social security for the growing numbers of older persons. In many societies, the expectation is that the family will take care of its economically dependent older members. While some families support their older relatives, others are not in a financial position to do so in a way that does not affect their own economic situation. Older persons who do not have family to support them are especially vulnerable. Today, older people are facing major challenges in their life. Thus, the need for social work intervention is likely to address the following challenges faced by the elderly.

First, as noted above, informal support systems for older persons are increasingly undergoing stress, as a consequence, among others, of lower fertility, out-migration of the young and women working outside the home. Elderly people fail to receive adequate support in their social environment.

Second, health is another major concern for older persons. The demographic transition to an ageing population, accompanied by an epidemiological transition from the predominance of infectious diseases to non-communicable diseases, is associated with an increasing demand for health care and long-term care.

Third, although not an inevitable outcome of growing old, the numbers of older people affected by mental health problems are increasing due to population ageing. Their management has become an increasing concern for both developing and developed countries. Maintaining good health and access to health care is a core concern of the older people everywhere. In many developed countries, quality of care and rising healthcare costs are major issues related to population ageing.

Fourth, financial security is one of the major concerns as people age. It is an issue for both older persons and a growing challenge for families and societies. There is an increasing consensus that countries must develop social protection systems that cover at least the basic needs of all older persons. Ensuring a secure income in old age is seen as a major challenge for governments facing fiscal problems and competing priorities.

Fifth, changing family and kinship structure of India is diminishing the capacity of the family to take care of its aged members which also a major area of concern because family is a basic unit of socialisation which provides social, emotional, and financial support to its old members.

Sixth, social workers challenge social injustice. Therefore to ensure fully exercising human and civil rights and equal opportunities, being free from discrimination, harassment, neglect, exploitation or abuse is yet another major challenge for social workers.

Seventh, maintaining good physical, emotional and mental health, personal dignity and respect, with opportunities for physical activity and access to appropriate treatment and to support in managing long-term conditions independently, keeping clean and comfortable in a chosen environment.

Other important aspects such as transition in role and relationships, and generation gap are also major challenges in front of the older people. Ensuring enabling and supportive environments, as people grow older is a significant challenge, so that older persons can age actively and participate in the political, social, economic and cultural life of society. Older persons, who find themselves in conflict situations, natural disasters—including those resulting from climate change—and other humanitarian emergencies, are particularly vulnerable. When younger generations migrate to cities or abroad, older persons are often left behind without traditional family support. They often become victims of neglect, violence and abuse because of increasing dependence.

In response to these challenges, the specific contribution of social work is to adopt a holistic approach in understanding the needs and difficulties of the individuals and the families in their social context, and to help them develop the solutions and achieve the outcomes that best fit their strengths, aspirations and preferences. Therefore, social work intervention can play a significant role in the care of the aged by addressing their diverse problems and challenges. In the present study, the relevance of social work intervention has been assessed in the different aspects of aged care such as physical, mental health, and support system.

2

Agencies and Approaches

That society is changing rapidly is well documented for. This changing social scenario is affecting the social and cultural fabric of the society. Every individual face some kind of problem in this changing social scenario in his/her adjustment. In the entire human life span, old age is the crucial part. In this age, several changes take place in every human being and that affects the role and status of the elderly in the society. One of the major changes is physical decline. A number of agencies and approaches remain responsible for catering to the care of the elderly. Some of these agencies and approaches include living arrangements/ conditions, care, physical or mental health, support system including family arrangements (nuclear and joint/extended family system), social environment and of course, social work intervention.

This book assesses the living conditions, which include physical, mental health and support system of the aged, and address the issues by introducing social work intervention.

OBJECTIVES

Central objective of this study is to assess the relevance of social work intervention in the care of the aged. To achieve this objective, the research embraces the overarching aims.

- To assess the living conditions of the aged in the existing social environment, which include the physical and mental health and support system from kith and kin,

- To examine the usefulness of social work intervention among the aged by addressing the issues emerging from their current living conditions,
- To determine the impact of social work intervention in the care of the aged, and
- To propose appropriate recommendations in the care of the aged based on the findings of the present study

REVIEWING THE LITERATURE

Notwithstanding, author's reflections on elderly peoples' agency and the issues linked to the care of the aged have been inspired by literature emanating from both the Anglo-American world and India. The research studies carried out in the field of old age by different scholars have been classified into following sub-sections:

Living Arrangements,
Physical Health,
Mental Health, and
Support System.

Living Arrangements

One of the most influential factors in the adjustment of the elderly is the environment in which they live in. Living arrangement is one of the most important environmental factors that affect the personal and social adjustments of the elderly. The current situation of the elderly can be identified from their living arrangements (Kumar Panda, 1998), and it should be treated as an important component of the general well-being of the elderly (Bali, 1996). Any study regarding the living arrangements of the elderly in India originates from the assumption of the declining joint family structure in the Indian society. In this context, Kumar (1991) observed, "nuclear families are being formed today, particularly in urban areas thereby causing much more concern about the living arrangement and social and economic support to the aged persons." The terms 'living arrangement', 'co-residence pattern' and 'residential arrangement' or 'residential pattern' are often used synonymously (Wall, 1989).

Usually the living arrangement of the elderly is understood in terms of the family type in which they live in, the headship they enjoy and with whom they stay, the kind of relationship they keep with their kith and kin, and on the whole, the extent to which they adjust to the changing environment. The family structure and the living arrangements of the individuals change as they pass through different stages of their life cycle. According to Hurlock (1975), the pattern of living arrangement varies much more in old age than in the middle age when the pattern is well standardised. Elderly living in old age home, an idea borrowed from the west, is a recent phenomenon in India. Though in the West, it is a common need for the elderly to seek help in institutions, even such communities are seriously considering the ill effects of institutionalization.

The survey of literature related to the living arrangements among the elderly reveals important dimensions, which have a bearing on the policies addressed to the welfare of the elderly. In this regard, changes in living arrangements, family structure and mode of retirement adversely affect the old people. Further, the old people are in increasing proportion losing the status and security once they used to enjoy in traditional Indian society.

With regard to the transformation in the Indian family system there are considerable overlap between the problems of widows and old-age in rural India; for an economically independent couple (with surviving spouse) the decision on co-residence with the children (sons in particular) is based on the situations and preferences of the older as well the younger generations. Also, there seems to be a differential situation between elderly people with and without surviving off-spring, no matter whether the elderly live with the surviving offspring or not. With regard to the elderly staying in nuclear families, few study found that the elderly in nuclear households had a feeling of helplessness. The aged are looked upon as a burden in barely sustainable, households in which every member contributes to the family earning. Therefore, household support towards elderly becomes very difficult among poverty-stricken households. An examination of intra-family relations of the urban elderly found that satisfactory intra-family relations were somewhat higher among the widows than the widowers were and somewhat lower among those living in joint families compared with those living in nuclear families. Further, those elderly who fail to bear substantial assets or a fairly good source of income and are economically dependent, find the attitude and behaviour of their family members unsatisfactory.

The National Sample Survey in 1991 found loneliness to be one of the major problems among the aged in India. Majority of the Indian elderly are without their spouse and live with their children or grandchildren. On examining the perception of the aged themselves on their status in the family and community in the wake of changing societal structure, it is found that the aged feel that they have lost status as a result of old age; a few others observed that they had lost status due to their retirement from work. A feeling was different between the sexes, as the women never had the feeling of being retired from work as against the men, whose status was associated with their work. The status of the aged in the changing social structure has been investigated by social scientists from different perspectives. Such investigations have more or less confirmed the breakdown of kinship and family organisations, which finds the elderly in a state of helplessness, isolation and economic dependence. Most of the primary surveys, which have investigated the preferences of the aged regarding their place of stay, have found that a majority prefer to stay with their children or family members in their old age.

In the absence of familial support, the elderly often prefer to stay in old-age homes provided they are economically affordable. In India, there are few old-age homes run by the state and central governments for the deprived and the poor elderly. The institutionalization of the aged has not become popular and these facilities are not accessible to the rural elderly. The inmates of the old-age homes expressed satisfaction with their stay there compared with their own homes. This finding gives the impression that old-age homes are serving as alternative caregivers to those who are unable to obtain familial care. Besides economic reasons, family quarrels were found to have induced the elderly to move into old-age homes.

This survey of literature shows that changing family structure in India has affected the well-being of the elderly by depriving them of the familial support of a traditional joint family setup and also due to the changing values and norms of the younger generation.

Physical Health

It is obvious that people become more and more susceptible to chronic diseases, physical disabilities and mental incapacities in their old age. As age advances, due to deteriorating physiological conditions, the body becomes more prone to illness. The illnesses of the elderly are multiple and chronic in nature. Arthritis, rheumatism, heart problems and high blood pressure are the most prevalent chronic diseases affecting them. Some of the health problems of the elderly can be attributed to social values also. The idea that old age is an age of ailments and physical infirmities is deeply rooted in the Indian mind and many of the sufferings and the elderly accept physical troubles, which are curable, as natural and inevitable. Regarding the health problems of the elderly of different socioeconomic status, it was found that while the elderly poor largely describe their health problems, on the basis of easily identifiable symptoms, like chest pain, shortness of breath, prolonged cough, breathlessness/asthma, eye problems, difficulty in movements, tiredness and teeth problems, the upper class elderly, in view of their greater knowledge of illnesses, mentioned blood pressure, heart attacks, and diabetes, which are largely diagnosed through clinical examination. NFHS-2 found the lifestyle adopted by the elderly and its effects on their health conditions. It was found that lifestyle adversely affects health and increases morbidity conditions among the elderly. Lifestyle habits such as alcohol consumption, regular smoking and tobacco chewing have adverse effects on one's ability to control diseases.

Social factors affecting the health of the elderly while there are no data showing direct relationship between income level and health of elderly individuals, one would assume that the nutritional and clinical care needs of the elderly are better met with adequate income than without it. If so, the poor countries and the poorer segments of the elderly population within each country would experience problems of health and well-being. The main area of concern among the elderly is their health, which can in turn have a significant impact on their economic security, level of independence and social interaction. The analysis of National Sample Survey (NSS) revealed that a huge majority (70%) of the elderly reporting their health status to be ranging from "excellent" to "good/fair" while around a quarter of the elderly reported their health to be poor. Previous analysis has uncovered that such a high percentage of positive assessment of health status was despite a large number of the elderly reporting to be suffering from at least one disability or chronic ailment. Their analysis throws light on the difference in self-reported health status across sex. Despite the female disadvantage in reported health status and preponderance of older women among immobile elderly, a much greater proportion of men are hospitalized as compared to their female counterparts (87 vs. 67 per 1000). The diseases among the elderly for which there are more hospitalized cases than the rest are heart diseases, cataract and bronchial asthma. Based on the observations made on the health status of India's elderly, it can be concluded that some definite health intervention is necessary to cater to specific complications in old age.

The rural elderly are mostly illiterate with low income. They suffer from more nutritional, physiological and other problems. The men are more literate, economically independent and face less physiological and nutritional problems as compared to their female counterparts. When the literacy level, income level and employment status improve, they seem to be more comfortable with their health conditions and living status.

Some clinical studies have found that multiplicities of diseases are normal among the elderly and that a majority of the old are often ill with chronic bronchitis, anaemia, hypertension, digestive troubles, rheumatism, scabies and fever. Some of the cases of disability among the elderly, as reported by a few medical studies, are difficulty in walking and standing, partial or complete blindness, partial deafness and difficulty in moving some joints, indigestion and mild breathlessness. The differential ageing phenomena, both physical and mental, appear to depend on environmental and social factors such as diet, type of education, adjustment to family and professional life, and consumption of tobacco and alcohol. Generally, when we compare the pre-and post-retirement situation of health of the retired, it is seen that if a retired person keeps himself/herself fit before and immediately after his/her retirement, he/she can be free from illness during the post-retirement period; but once an illness starts, before or just after the retirement, he/she continues to face it during the post-retirement period. A recently conducted medico-social study of the urban elderly in Mumbai has revealed that the influence of the factors such as educational status, economic status, age, marital status, perception on living status, addictions, degree of feeling idle, anxieties and worries, type of health center visited and whether or not taking medicines, on both the perceived and actual health status of the elderly is found to be significant and varies considerably across different classes and sexes of the elderly.

At an advanced age, due to restricted physical activity, a majority of the elderly change their living habits, especially their dietary intake and duration of sleep. There is a general perception in the community that since the old age lead a sedentary life, they should eat less food, have more rest and develop more interest in religion to occupy them. Several factors like lack of physical movement, absence of a work routine, ill-health, etc. are observed to be responsible for irregularity in the sleeping schedule of the elderly. The allocation of less time to sleep among the lower strata of the elderly probably indicates the compulsions for them to work. Besides, inadequate facilities in the household go against resting or sleeping during the day. The wide differences observed among the male and female elderly in this stratum is probably due to greater prevalence of health problems, compulsions to continue in labour force, and the resultant stress and worries about unfinished tasks, which the male elderly mostly face.

There appears to be a significant difference in the health situation of the elderly living in the rural areas in comparison to those living in the urban areas. The elderly people living in the rural areas appear to be much healthier as compared to those residing in the urban areas. Interestingly, the prevalence of chronic disease among females is higher than that among the males in the case of urban areas while reverse is the case in rural areas. The prevalence of various types of physical disabilities was found to be quite high among the elderly. All types of disabilities were also found to be more prevalent in rural areas as compared to the urban areas. Very large majority of the elderly suffer from curtailed functional abilities in physical (eating, bathing, dressing, walking, climbing stairs, getting-up from a sitting position, etc.) as well as in sensory (hearing and vision) health domains. These illnesses force them to rely on formal or informal help in their day-to-day activities.

These problems of incapacitation are found to be particularly acute among the lower income groups. Women are the worst sufferers, with less of filial support. Social policy of the developing countries like India underplays the healthcare requirements of the elderly, especially elderly women. Another study wherein two sub-sample surveys were conducted by Ramamurthy and Jamuna shows the utilization pattern of various available health services and assesses the impact of the geriatric services made available. It indicates that while lessons are to be learnt from the experiences of the West, the policies to be adopted by India need to be geared to existing factors like changes in beliefs and practices, relative responsibility of the kin and the community, values attached to the health and the elderly. Mere availability of the services does not ensure its utilization. The knowledge and understanding of the services available, accessibility of the services and willingness to utilize the services are some of the important factors playing a role. In assessing healthcare services delivery, it is important to note the load of disease, the availability of existing services and their capability to handle this existing load, to identify the areas that need strengthening and the lacunae that need to be fulfilled. It is clear from the above review of earlier studies on health of the elderly that the health and well-being of the elderly are affected by many interwoven aspects of their social and physical environment. Family support is found to be an important factor for socio-psychological well-being of the elderly. These range from their lifestyle and family structure to social and economic support systems, to the organisation and provision of health care. The pattern of various inputs for developing the appropriate social policy for the welfare of the elderly may have to be suitably modified in view of the diversity of the factors and their differential influence on the living conditions of the elderly.

Apparently, health status is a contingent condition that greatly facilitates the process of adjustment. The problem of mobility increases with age. The aged people do not have much knowledge about various age related diseases. This, in turn, influences their health attitudes and practices. On this dimension, rural elderly are relatively worse off in health awareness than their urban counterparts are.

Therefore, this survey of literature shows that physical health has affected the well-being of the elderly, which raises the need of elderly care and protection at this crucial stage of human life cycle.

Mental Health

Mental health of the elderly is another important factor in understanding their overall health situation. It is generally expected that the elderly should be free from mental worries since they have already completed their share of tasks and should lead a peaceful life. However, often the unfinished familial tasks like education of children, marriage of daughter(s), etc. become a source of worry over a period of time. It is noticed that the worries among the poor are usually about inadequate economic support, poor health, inadequate living space, loss of respect, unfinished familial tasks, lack of recreational facilities and the problem of spending time. In an epidemiological study on dementia in

Maharashtra with 2145 randomly selected respondents, the prevalence of dementia in the community was seen to be 4.1 per cent and the risk of dementia increases more than five-fold in the oldest old. It is presumed that such differences narrow down as socioeconomic status of the elderly increases because with higher education and income they would have greater access to health/ medical information and services. There is a general perception among the elderly that they are prone to illnesses mainly due to their advanced age and that it is natural to suffer from such health problems. However, in reality, most of their diseases are minor in nature and curable at the initial stage itself. Most of them neglect the illnesses and postpone seeking medical aid. In some cases, due to neglect of timely medication, the health problems become aggravated and sometimes lead to death. Although the retired persons enjoy the benefit of pensions, a large number of the elderly in India, who do not belong to the 'employed' category, do not enjoy any social security benefits. During the service period, certain medical facilities such as free treatment and supply of medicines from the government hospitals/ dispensaries are provided to the employees. However, these facilities are not available after retirement, when the old people are really in need of such subsidies. Thus, retired government servants face a hard time after retirement if they are suffering from any serious illness.

Among the aged population, the magnitude of mental morbidity in India is nearly 4 million. This is a serious cause of concern when seen in the context of woefully low psychiatric services. Certain mental signs of old age among the older people as loss in concentration or attention, loss of recent memory, development of religious sentiments, frustrations, depression, weakening of reflexes, etc. The older people having failed to achieve their goals earlier in life become bitter, disappointed, and cynical. They blame others for their failures and remain depressed and unhappy. Fein son (1986) in his study finds chief mental problems, among the aged, as mental tension (88%), fear of death (74.5%), feeling of dependency (71%), anxiety (70%), loneliness (62.5%), helplessness (60%), depression (52.5%) and feeling of uselessness (52%). Feinson (1986) finds that the older females have greater psychological impairment than their male counterparts do. On the level of anxiety, 61 per cent of elderly score low, 25 per cent average and 4 per cent high. Women are reported to have anxiety more than men do. About 41 per cent aged respondents are pessimistic, 38 per cent balanced and 22 per cent optimistic. Study brings out that those retirees who stay cognitively active and also those who feel themselves younger recall significantly more materials than those who re-cognitively inactive.

Therefore, this survey of literature shows serious cause for mental health, which needs a treatment and preventive approach for the well-being of the older people.

Support System

In recent years, social network and social support have become increasingly important concepts in gero-psychology. Caplan (1974) defines social support in terms of human attachment, which promotes mastery of emotions, offers guidance, provides feedback and validates identity. Cobb (1976) viewed it as information from others that one is loved, respected, esteemed, and involved. It encompasses a whole range of care, support and services. According to him, social network is a set of people with whom an elderly maintains contact and has some form of bond. Bowling *et al.* (1991) distinguished social network from social support and defined social support as the interactive process in which emotional, instrumental or financial aid is obtained from one's social network. Considering the Indian elderly, explained social support in terms of concern and assistance from the family, community and from other social institutions. With the support, the elderly may feel that there are significant people who are concerned about them in times of crisis. Support network to an elderly person is available from both the formal and informal sources. However, in India, like in other developing countries, only a limited formal support system exists. In general, the family is the most significant support network for the elderly. Family support for the elderly is believed to be culturally determined and socially reinforced (Gangrade, 1989). Like other third world countries, the Indian culture emphasises on the family support and the care for the aged. There are a few theories concerning the informal support networks of the elderly. These theories highlight the importance and uniqueness of the family as a support system for the elderly. The key factor that determines who provides which form of support is the primacy of the relationship. This model assumes that among the elderly people, kin are usually the first choice, followed by friends and other formal institutions. Another model, 'task specific model' emphasises on both the nature of the task performed and features of the persons in the support network. This model highlights the uniqueness of primary groups. According to this model, some persons are best suited than others for meeting specific tasks, rather than all tasks, as posited by the hierarchical compensation model. It regards family as the most appropriate group for providing extensive long-term emotional and instrumental support. Weiss (1974) proposed 'functional specificity of relationship model', which views relationships that emphasise task or need specialisation, but is less concerned with specifying which person will satisfy which need. However, the results of an empirical test of the functional specificity model indicated that, among the elderly persons, spouse and children are the key source of aid and security, spouse is the primary source of intimacy while participation in a group is primarily a source of self-esteem. This model emphasises the diversity of social network for the elderly.

The family as a system, along with its elder members, confronts major adaptational challenges in later life: stresses of widowhood, retirement, grandparenthood, illness, all require family support. As an informal support system for the aged, the family can serve as a resource by helping with their instrumental needs (Wenger, 1984; Antonucci, 1990) and by providing emotional support (Antonucci, 1990). In general, these research shows that the family members are more likely to provide older adults with instrumental support than others, even friends, when the needs are significant and chronic, and older adults even express a preference for support from kin over friends, neighbours or others. The family structures, through network linkage, activities and interaction provide intimacy and human worth, and both are requisites for the survival and quality of living of the aged. It also serves as a buffer between stress, physical and mental impairment. The absence of family members may limit access to support within some domains, especially in later life when overall network size is reduced (Carstensen & Lang, 1994). Importance of family relationships and familial ties in the lives of old people are very much stressed in gerontological literature. Researchers suggest that satisfactory family relationships are salient in late adulthood. They are related to one's life satisfaction and play a dominant role in identity preservation. There is abundant evidence that family ties have remained important for the elderly despite the changes in the family pattern.

A satisfying husband-wife relationship contributes to good adjustment and happiness in old age. Most of the western studies on marital relationships across the family life cycle indicated marital satisfaction as 'curvilinear', high among young couples, declining after the birth of the first child through the launching stage and then increasing during the post-parental stage. Simultaneously, others (Blood & Wolf, 1960) showed marital satisfaction either reaching a plateau or declining after the birth of the first child. An increase in marital satisfaction in later years was reported by many researchers (Anderson *et al.*, 1983) and one study (Gilford, 1984) concluded that older couples experience a 'honeymoon phase' after retirement. According to them, when a man completes 60 years of age, the event is celebrated as 'second honeymoon'. This stage involves a rediscovery of each other and reestablishment of an intimate abiding relationship. However, the issue of marital satisfaction in later life is hotly debated and remains unresolved.

Another most frequently encountered observation in the literature of the family life of the elderly is the important role of children in their lives. The quality of parent-child relationships assessed by variables, such as communication and affection, is positively related to parental psychological well-being in their ageing process. However, memories of family problems from earlier years can affect the quality of relationship between adult children and parents (Webster & Herozog, 1995). Recently, the researchers are recognising the impact of satisfying interpersonal relationships and intergenerational interactions on adjustment of elderly. Parent child relations in later life are increasingly determined by factors such as basic trust, respect, shared values, beliefs and social class. There are gender, marital status and social class differences in patterns of family contacts in old age. It is well documented in the literature that women are likely to take responsibility to maintain contact within the family over the life cycle, a pattern that continues well into old age. Widowers establish more family contact than the married elderly (Field *et al.*, 1993) and widows, particularly living alone, have more frequent contact with their children, most frequently with a daughter (Shanas *et al.*, 1968). There are also social class differences in the pattern of family contact and support (Bayer & Woods, 1963; Adams, 1968, Shanas *et al.*, 1968). In the Indian family set up, spouse, married or unmarried children and daughters-in-law are significant and salient in the lives of the elderly. However, due to several reasons, the interactions and relationships between family members and the elderly may not be as satisfying; at least in some cases, the relationships may be strained. Again, the relationship between the mother-in-law and the daughter-in-law is crucial in determining the satisfaction of the elderly. The traditional stigma attached to mother-in-law and daughter-in-law relationship, often affects the care giving relationship negatively. Moreover, the level of interaction in the past and the personality of the mother-in-law are some other factors that determine the quality of relationships and care. Hence, in a care giving relationship, the son-father and mother-in-law and daughter-in-law equations are forces that determine the quality of relationship and the care that the old members receive in the family environment.

Though co-residence is an important criterion for the well-being of the elderly, it may not always ensure a healthy relationship between successive generations. The economic, emotional, and social support from the younger generation may be provided even without co-residence. However, given the level of socio-economic development and the absence of an institutional support system for the elderly in the country, it is unlikely that such support may be provided by a majority of the children to their parents. Similarly, co-residence does not always indicate flow of support from the younger to the older generation; co-residence may also imply child-care or help in household chores by the elderly.

Hence, survey of literature showed that changing living arrangements and declining health status of older people affects the support system of the elderly. There is an urgent need of aged care, which can facilitate the elderly people in their social functioning. In the next sections, I discuss the methodological approaches deployed for this research.

RESEARCH DESIGN, APPROACH AND THE STUDY AREA

In order to evaluate the impact of social work intervention in the care of the aged, the research used pre-test post-test non-equivalent control group design of quasi-experimental research designs.

Many a times it is not possible to achieve random assignments of subjects to experimental and control groups and with holds intervention to one group (control group). In such cases, instead of foregoing the study altogether, it is sometimes possible to create and execute alternative research designs. These designs are called quasi-experimental research designs and are distinguished from experimental research designs due to lack of random assignments of subjects to experimental and control groups (Lal Das, 2010). When we try to get an existing control group (comparison group) that appears to be similar to the experimental group that research design is commonly called as pre-test post-test non-equivalent control group design and symbolised as follows:

E→Y1→ X→Y2

C→Y'1→Non-X→Y'2

Where:

E → Experimental Group

C → Control Group

Y1 → Dependent Variable before introduction of X (Pre-Test)
X → Intervention
Non-X → No Intervention
Y2 → Dependent Variable after introduction of X (Post-Test)

As previously mentioned, the study was carried out in two villages namely, *Madwana* was selected as an experimental village (*Mall* Block) and *Goila* as a control village (*Bakshi Ka Talab* Block) of Lucknow district in Uttar Pradesh. *Madwana* is the remote village as compared to *Goila* and also backward in comparison of other social and economic indicators. Hence, it was decided to hold the intervention in *Madwana* and keep *Goila* as a control village.

Lucknow, the capital city, is one of the major metropolitan cities of India. It has always been known as a multicultural city, which flourished as a cultural and artistic hub of North India in the 18th and the 19th centuries. Today, it continues as an important centre of government, education, culture, tourism, music and poetry. *Goila* and *Madwana* are respectively situated approximately 30 and 50 kilometers away from the Lucknow city. The total population of *Goila* and *Madwana* is 7,945 and 4393 respectively. The schedule caste (SC) population in *Goila* is around 2253 while in *Madwana* they comprise 2159 people (Census of India, 2011). *Goila* has more population than *Madwana* while geographically *Madwana* is wider than *Goila*. According to the Census of India 2011, UP has a population of 199,581,477. Among them 77.72 per cent reside in the villages (rural sector) whereas 22.28 per cent live in towns or urban sectors. Both the villages have similar socio-cultural milieu. Basic means of commuting is motorcycle and bicycle. Traditional rituals, practices, culture, etc. are some of the key determining factors of these villages. Both the villages have a patriarchal structure. Many members of the extended families live together but are able to portray a nuclear family structure by maintaining a separate kitchen. Girls get married at an early age at about the age of 16. Working women, part of the farm labour, who belongs to the SC community and earn daily wages appear to be better off in comparison to women from traditionally land holding families in both the villages. Additionally, these working women are also for their embroidery and *chikan* works to support their family. When it comes to educational opportunities, the boys are given more importance than the girls are. The villagers have diverse cultural profile in their dressing, living style, food, habits, customs and traditions, rituals, mores, values and beliefs.

DATA COLLECTION

All the elderly within the rural and the urban sector of Lucknow District in Uttar Pradesh comprise the universe of the study.

Sample Size and Sampling Procedure

A total of 80 elderly (40 from each village) in the age group of 60 years and above (Figure: Chart 2.1) were taken as a sample size of the elderly. Social and gender representation was considered while choosing the sample. Various sampling methods were adopted at each stage for drawing 80 elderly respondents. The first stage was the selection of the district. Purposive sampling was applied in selection of the district. Hence, the Lucknow was purposively selected as a district. The present study had a six months intervention, so for the convenience of the study, the researcher selected this district to reduce economic burden as he belongs to this area.

Second stage of the sampling was the selection of the community development Blocks. Out of the eight blocks in the district, two blocks (*Bakshi Ka Talab* and *Mall*) were selected randomly.

Third stage of the sampling was the selection of the two villages. From each Block, one *Gram Panchayat* was randomly selected, thus, two *Panchayats* from the two Blocks were included in the sample. Each *Gram Panchayat* has its own *Gram Sabhas*. *Gram Sabha* was treated as a village and forms the basic unit of the sampling. *Goila* and *Madwana* were the two villages selected respectively from *Bakshi Ka Talab* and *Mall* Block. Lastly, through random sample method 40 elderly were selected from each village by doing transect walk to ensure the representation from all the sections of the society.

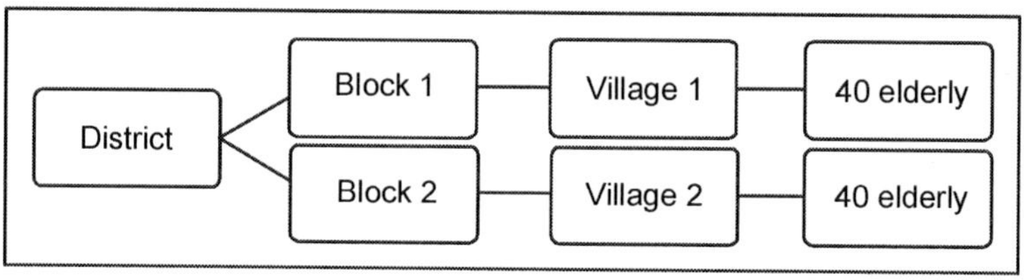

Chart 2.1: Size of Sample

Methods of Data Collection

The present study is experimental in nature as it seeks to experiment the social work intervention in the care of the aged. The study was designed to assess the living conditions of the aged in the existing social environment followed by six months social work intervention in the experimental village from October 2013 to March 2014 among the aged by addressing the issues emerging from their current living conditions. A post intervention study was also carried out to gauge the relevance of social work intervention in both the villages. Various methods were applied in the present study for data collection. Data was collected from the two sources: primary and secondary. Primary data was collected through interview schedule, case studies, Direct Intervention, and observations. A comprehensive interview schedule was developed to obtain data from the respondents during Pre and Post Intervention. Direct Intervention and Observation were used as a tool of data collection as the researcher stayed at experimental village and gather the information directly though intervention and observation. Home visits were also made to collect data through interview schedule. A huge range of secondary data was reviewed and accessed through various sources such as national and international publications in the form of books, journals and articles, magazine, newspapers, reports and thesis.

Process of Data Collection

Primary data was collected through direct interactions with the respondents. Before, embarking on the research, the researcher printed the interview schedule. The pre-intervention fieldwork for data collection was started from the *Goila* village because it was nearer to the city. During the pre-intervention phase, and as mentioned above, the researcher collected data from 80 respondents, 40 from each *Goila* and *Madwana*. Subsequently, the data was analysed and existing problems of the elderly were assessed in both the villages. As per the design of the study, the researcher started social work intervention in the experimental (*Madwana*) village for addressing the existing problems by introducing social work intervention. Thus, *Goila* remained as a control village. After six months of intervention, the researcher collected data from both the villages by applying the various tools of data collection. For secondary data, the various libraries in Delhi were visited. Besides, some institutions working on the elderly were also visited. In addition, the IGNOU library and its e-resource helped tremendously in secondary data collection. The data was also gathered from the Ministry of Social Justice and Empowerment, Census of India, and other relevant websites. The data processing and data analysis was done using computation of certain indices along with searching for patterns of relationship that exist among the data groups.

In the next chapter, the situational analysis of the elderly from both the villages during the pre-intervention phase is discussed.

3

Caring for the Elderly

Using a Pre-Intervention Assessment

In this empirical chapter, a baseline or pre-intervention assessment in order to evaluate the existing situation of the elderly has been applied. Situational analysis of the elderly is significant to develop an intervention strategy that aims at modification of the existing conditions of the elderly. Indeed, the pre-intervention assessment is used as a basis from which to compare the condition of the elderly after intervention has been introduced. By doing so, the chapter elucidates the situation of the respondents from both the villages during the pre-intervention phase.

DEMOGRAPHIC AND SOCIO-ECONOMIC CHARACTERISTICS

As stated elsewhere, 40 participants in the age group 60 and above, who gave their consents to participate in the research were selected from each of the two villages of *Goila* and *Madwana*. Each member had a distinct and unique characteristic. The demographic and socio-economic characteristics of the respondents are as follows:

Age

Age is an important variable on the basis of which all societies make assumptions about the appropriate behaviours and levels of functioning of people. In ancient and medieval era, respect was ascribed to any and every person higher in age. Hence, grey hair would bring a unique authority and power to a person in family and community (Panda, 2005).

In this research, the age of the respondents' ranges between 60 to 91 years in *Goila* while in *Madwana* it ranges between 60 to 94 years. The respondents were classified to facilitate further analysis into various sub-groups on the basis of their age, that is, 60-69 years, 70-79 years, 80-89 years, and 90 years and above. Table 3.1 shows that about 35 per cent of the respondents from *Goila* and 40 per cent from *Madwana* belong to the age group of 60-69 years. This table also reveals that approximately 13 per cent of the respondents from *Goila* and 10 per cent of the respondents from *Madwana* belong to the age group of 90 years and above.

Table 3.1: Distribution of the Elderly by Age Group

Sl.	Age Group	Goila (%)	Madwana (%)
1.	60-69	35.00	40.00
2.	70-79	30.00	25.00
3.	80-89	22.50	25.00
4.	> / = 90	12.50	10.00
	Total	**100.00**	**100.00**

Gender

With respect to gender, the research embraces 50 per cent male and 50 per cent female respondents from each village. Data in Table 3.2 unveils that approximately 18 per cent of the male respondents from *Goila* and *Madwana each* belong to the age group of 70-79 years while about 20 per cent of the female respondents from *Goila* and 25 per cent from *Madwana* belong to the age group of 60-69 years.

Marital Status

It is well documented that marriage assumes critical importance for

Table 3.2: Distribution of the Elderly by Gender

Sl.	*Age Group*	*Gender*	
		Male (%)	Female (%)
Goila			
1.	60-69	15.00	20.00
2.	70-79	17.50	12.50
3.	80-89	12.50	10.00
4.	> / = 90	5.00	7.50
	Total	**50.00**	**50.00**
Madwana			
1.	60-69	15.00	25.00
2.	70-79	17.50	7.50
3.	80-89	15.00	10.00
4.	> / = 90	2.50	7.50
	Total	**50.00**	**50.00**
	Overall	**100.00**	**100.00**

older people. That said, it is arguable that for the elderly, the marriage relationship is an important source of both socio-emotional and economic support. However, married elderly and widowed elderly experience ageing differently (Ward, 1979). Because of commitments and emotional investments, some relationships come to be viewed as unique, fragile, irreplaceable, and nontransferable (McCall and Simmons, 1966). Older people lose other roles and relationships when children leave home and with retirement, and limited physical mobility may restrict the range of relationships providing fulfillment of their interpersonal needs. Widowhood is therefore, a potentially critical aspect of the ageing experience (Ward, 1979). In the present study, the marital status of the respondents is classified into three categories such as married (living with spouse), widow, and widower. Chart 3.1illustrates that more than half of the respondents, that is, 60 per cent and 50 per cent are married and living with spouse respectively in Goila and Madwana. Data reveals that about 25 per cent of the respondents are widows in Goila whereas about 30 per cent of the respondents are widows in Madwana. Besides, the study also found substantial proportion of the widowers. Older women, particularly, widows should be high priority targets of social policies, given their vulnerability to low income, poor health, neglect, and abuse.

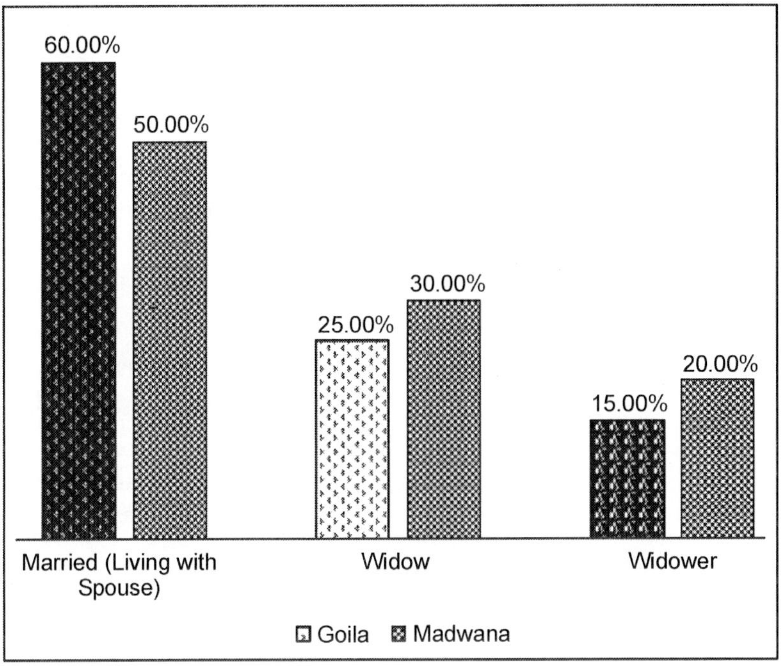

Chart 3.1: Distribution of the Elderly by Marital Status

Religion

Malinowski (1958) explicates that religion is a mode of action as well as a system of beliefs, a sociological phenomenon as well as a personal. Often two aspects of religion are identified such as spiritual and ritual. The former provides sustenance to value system, and the latter, an element of cohesiveness in-group living. With advancing age, many aged persons increasingly become ritualistic. Gangrade (1988) asserts that such rituals as family worship and festivals provide the elderly much social satisfaction as diversion from routine and monotony. The present study finds that all the respondents belong to two religions: *Hindu* and

Muslim. Data in Chart 3.2 unveils that majority of the respondents in *Goila* (80%) and *Madwana* (75%) belong to *Hindu* whereas about 20 per cent of the respondents in *Goila* and 25 per cent in *Madwana* are *Muslim*.

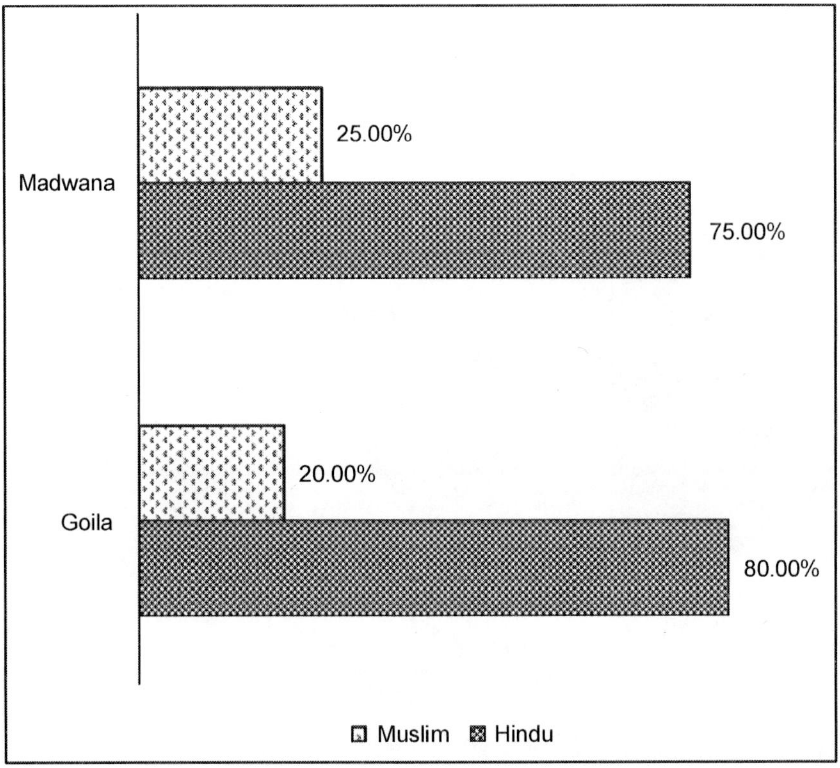

Chart 3.2: Distribution of the Elderly by Religion

Caste

Caste system is a unique characteristic of *Hindu* society. This age-old institution has stratified the society into four *varnas*: *Brahmin*, *Kashtriya*, *Vaishya* and *Shudra*. Since independence, Government of India has tried to improve the situation of the underprivileged sections, officially termed as Schedule Castes (SC), Schedule Tribes (ST) and Other Backward Classes (OBC) through several affirmative actions (Panda, 2005). In the study, respondents were found from three diverse caste categories such as General, OBC, and SC. The study found that the respondents from General and SC category are more as compared to OBC category in each village. Study showed that the respondents from General category are about 38 per cent in *Goila* and 35 per cent in *Madwana.* The representation of respondents from SC category is similar to the General category respondents in both the villages.

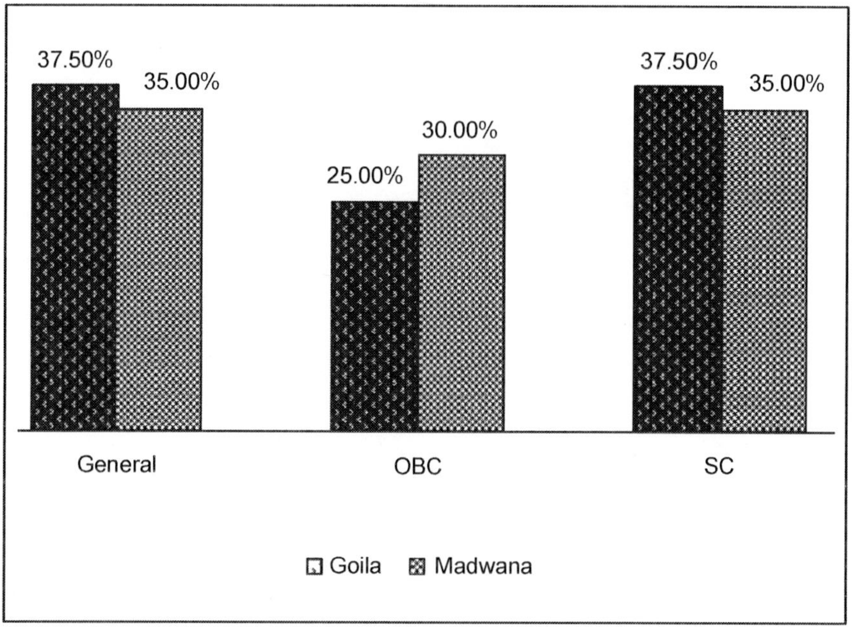

Chart 3.3: Distribution of the Elderly by Caste

Educational Status

One of the famous proverbs of Aristotle states, "Education is the best provision in old age." In this study, the respondents were having various levels of education such as elementary, high school and intermediate. There was significant proportion of the illiterate respondents in both the villages that is, *Goila* (40%) and *Madwana* (35%). Chart 3.4 shows that majority of the respondents (48%) had attained their education up to the elementary level in *Goila* and *Madwana* respectively.

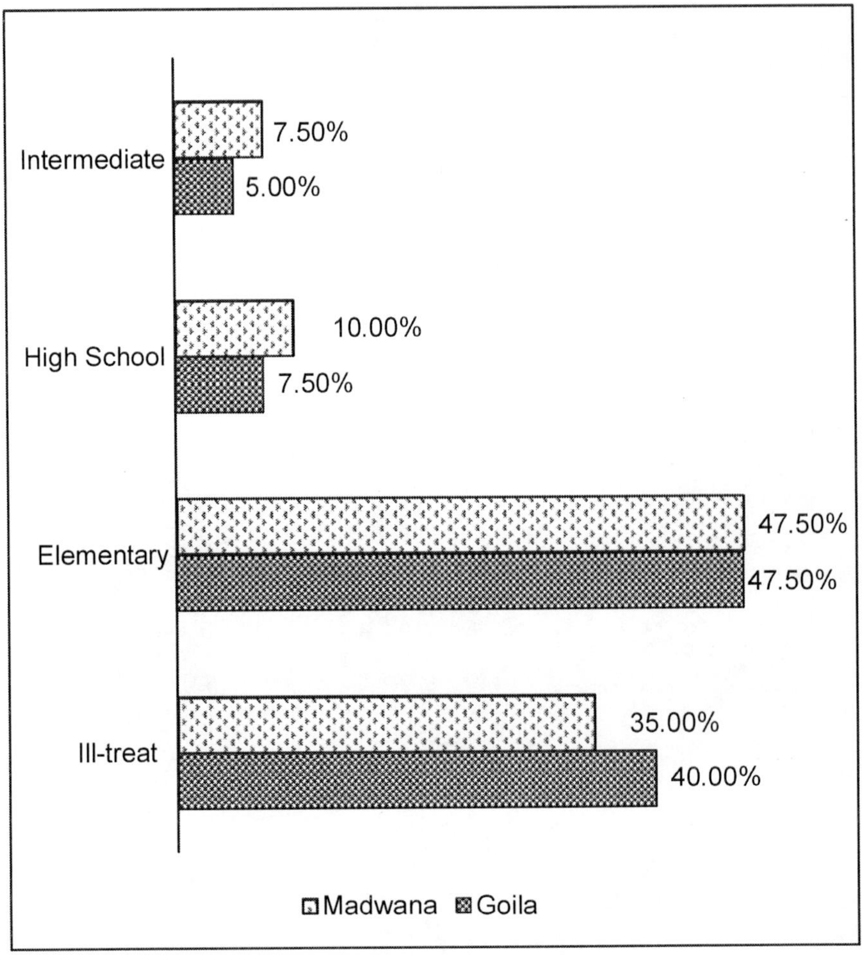

Chart 3.4: Distribution of the Elderly by their Educational Status

Occupation

Occupational status, many a times, gives an indication of the economic position, self-confidence and life-style of an individual. In this study the respondents were engaged in mainly two types of occupation: agriculture and daily wage labour. About 48 per cent of the respondents in *Goila* and 45 per cent in *Madwana* were without work. Agriculture is the major occupation of the respondents in both the villages. Data in Chart 3.5 shows that about 38 per cent of the respondents in *Goila* and 35 per cent in *Madwana* are engaged in agriculture.

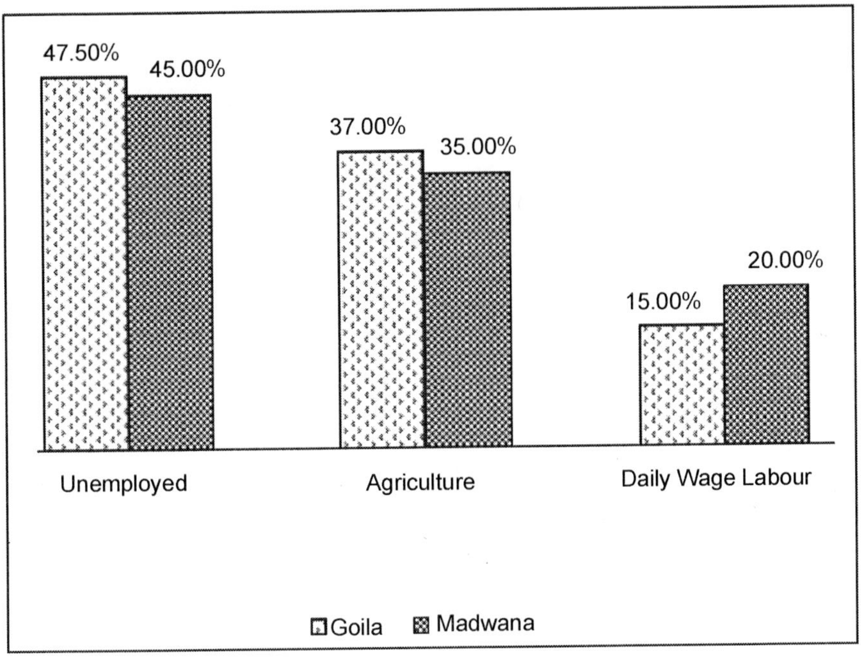

Chart 3.5: Distribution of the Elderly by their Occupational

Monthly Income

Three categories of income group were found, that is, no income, income less than Rs. 1500, and income in between Rs. 1500 to 3000. As the study is on aged population, it well implies that majority of the respondents have no income. They were dependent on their families, kith and kin. Chart 3.6 shows that 48 per cent of the respondents in Goila and 45 per cent of the respondents in Madwana are unemployed. Data reveals that the monthly income of approximately 38 per cent of the respondents in Goila and 35 per cent in Madwana are in between Rs. 1500 to 3000.

BASIC AMENITIES

Housing Type

The villagers live in two types of houses. First, the house which is

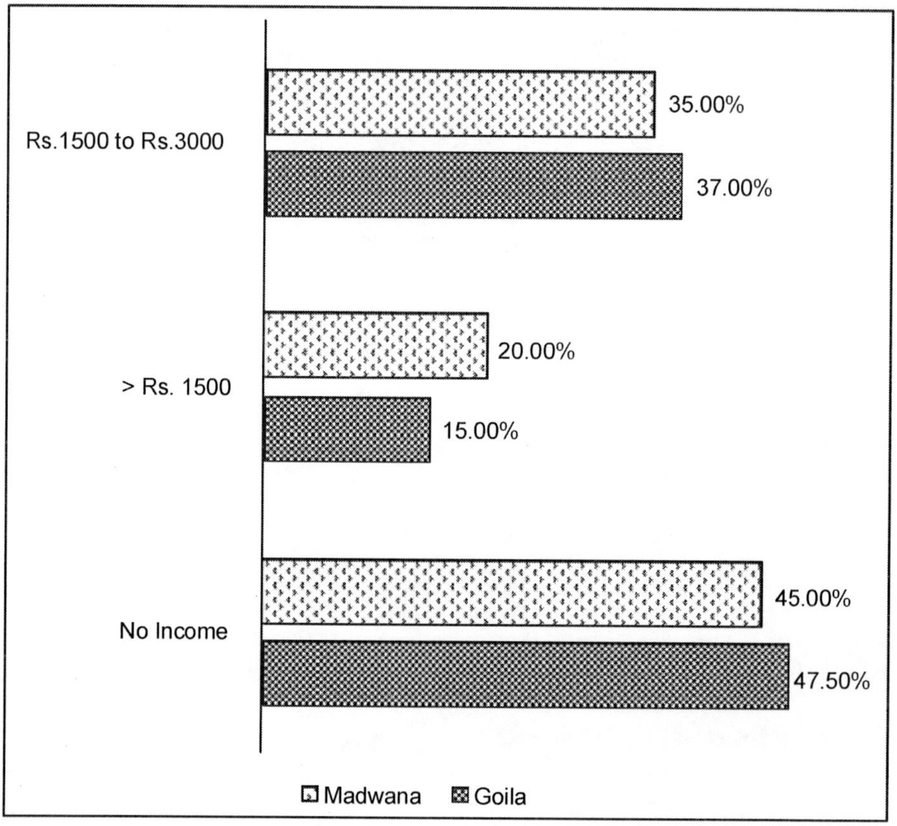

Chart 3.6: Distribution of the Elderly by their Monthly Income

constructed by them or their family members called own house. Second, the house, which is constructed by government's financial support, called government provided house. Data in Chart 3.7 showed that majority of the respondents in *Goila* (85%) and *Madwana* (88%) live in their own houses. This is because the respondents with their rise in age (with their mental and physical health in the decline) want to live comfortably for the rest of their life in their own house. However, 15 per cent of the respondents in *Goila* and 13 per cent in *Madwana* live in government provided houses.

Drinking Water Facility

With regards to the availability of drinking water facility majority of

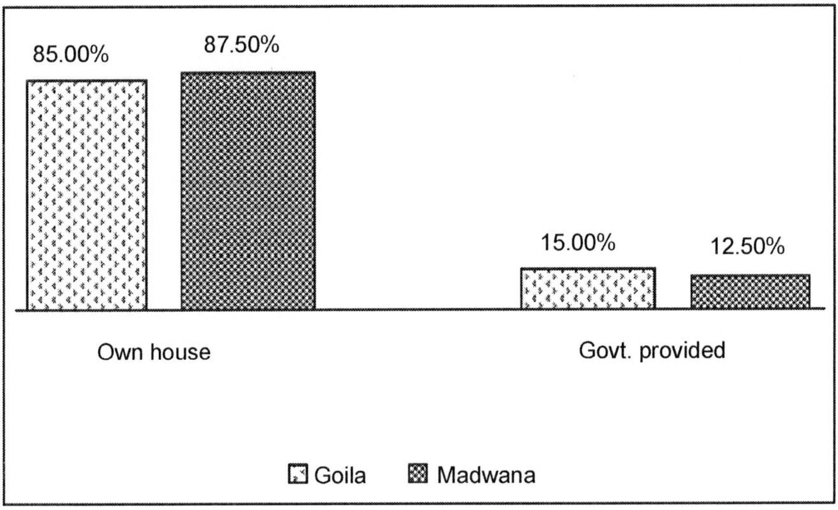

Chart 3.7: Distribution of the Elderly by their Housing Type

the respondents' utilize government hand pumps. Chart 3.8 reveals that about 70 per cent of the respondents in *Goila* and 65 per cent in *Madwana* are dependent on government hand pumps, whereas 30 per cent respondents in *Goila* and 35 per cent in *Madwana* are having their own hand pumps. Therefore, majority of the elderly face challenges even for the basic requirements as drinking water.

Toilet Facility

Majority of the respondents do not have the toilet facility at their houses. Data in Table 3.3 shows that only 28 per cent of the respondents in *Goila* and 35 per cent in *Madwana* are availing the toilet facility at their houses. Physically frail elderly belonging to 70 years and above generally face the trouble in going to the toilet outside.

GOVERNMENT PENSION

The shift in age structure makes issues difficult for social security and economic support for the elderly. There are government provisions for the older people where they can avail the old age and widow pension.

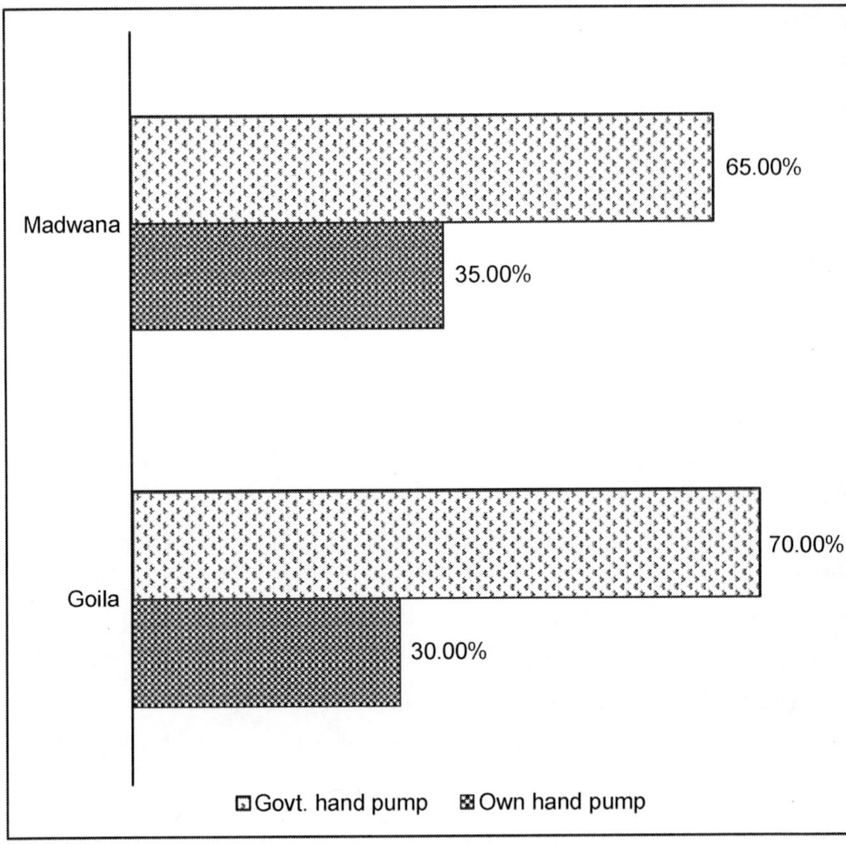

Chart 3.8: Availability of Drinking Water Facility for the Elderly

Table 3.3: Number of Elderly Having Toilet Facility by Age Group

Sl.	Age Group	Goila (%)	Madwana (%)
1.	60-69	10.00	12.50
2.	70-79	7.50	10.00
3.	80-89	5.00	7.50
4.	> / = 90	5.00	5.00
	Total	**27.50**	**35.00**

Though majority of the respondents were eligible in both the villages for receiving the old age and widow pension but failed to have any access. Table 3.4 unveils that about 5 per cent of the respondents in *Goila* and 10 per cent in *Madwana* could avail the old age pension. There were no beneficiaries of widow pension in both the villages whereas

Table 3.4: Numbers of Elderly Receiving Government Pension

Sl.	*Pension*	*Goila (%)*	*Madwana (%)*
1.	Old Age Pension	5.00	10.00
2.	Widow Pension	0.00	0.00
	Total	**5.00**	**10.00**

about 25 per cent of respondents in *Goila* and 30 per cent in *Madwana* are widows.

LIVING ARRANGEMENTS

Type of Family

The living arrangements of the respondents are extremely diverse. Most elderly people considered for this research reside with their family members, spouses, relatives, and even alone. Table 3.5 reveals that about 38 per cent of the respondents in *Goila* and 28 percent in *Madwana* reside in joint family. A total of 23 per cent of the respondents in *Goila* and 28 per cent in *Madwana* reside with their spouses and about 8 per cent of the respondents in *Goila* and 10 per cent in *Madwana* live alone.

Table 3.5: Type of Family of the Elderly

Sl.	*Type*	*Goila (%)*	*Madwana (%)*
1.	Joint Family	37.50	27.50
2.	Nuclear Family	20.00	25.00
3.	With Spouse	22.50	27.50
4.	With Relatives	12.50	10.00
5.	Alone	7.50	10.00
	Total	**100.00**	**100.00**

Accommodation

The research unfolds that the place where the elderly reside is segregated into three types of accommodation: separate, shared, and unfixed. Some of the respondents (30% in *Goila* and 23% in *Madwana*) have separate place to live while a considerable number of the respondents do not have a fixed accommodation to reside. Table 3.6 paints that about half of the respondents have shared accommodation in both the villages.

Table 3.6: Accommodation of the Elderly

Sl.	Type	Goila (%)	Madwana (%)
1.	Separate	30.00	22.50
2.	Shared	50.00	52.50
3.	Unfixed Place	20.00	25.00
	Total	**100.00**	**100.00**

Food Arrangement

Their spouses, daughter(s) in law and relatives arrange the food for the respondents. Some of the respondents arrange their food by themselves. Data in Table 3.7 shows that 35 per cent of the respondents in *Goila* and 38 per cent in *Madwana* prepare their own meal. About 30 per cent of the respondents in *Goila* and 20 per cent in *Madwana* are dependent for food on their daughter in laws. Study also revealed that about 20 per cent of the respondents in *Goila* and 28 per cent in *Madwana* are dependent for food on their spouses. The study found that food is arranged by the relatives for the significant proportion of the respondents in both the villages.

Table 3.7: Food Arrangements for the Elderly

Sl.	Arranged by	Goila (%)	Madwana (%)
1.	Spouse	20.00	27.50
2.	Self	35.00	37.50
3.	Daughter in Law	30.00	20.00
4.	Relatives	15.00	15.00
	Total	**100.00**	**100.00**

Leisure Time

Leisure activities of advantaged and disadvantaged older people differ depending upon the availability of resources. It varies from person to person and is influenced by one's age, culture and standing in society. In *Goila* and *Madwana*, respondents like to spend their leisure time mostly with spouses, family members, relatives, friends, neighbours, and children. Significant proportions of the respondents live alone during their leisure time as well. Data in Table 3.8 reveals that about 33 per cent of the respondents in *Goila* and 30 per cent in *Madwana* spend their leisure time with their family members and relatives. The study also shows that around 13 per cent of the respondents, in both *Goila* and *Madwana* spend their leisure time with their spouses. Besides, this study also found that about 28 per cent of the respondents in *Goila* and 20 per cent in *Madwana* spend their leisure time with their friends and neighbours.

Table 3.8: Elderly Spending the Leisure Time

Sl.	*Spent With*	*Goila (%)*	*Madwana (%)*
1.	Spouse	12.50	12.50
2.	Family Members and Relatives	32.50	30.00
3.	Friends and Neighbours	27.50	20.00
4.	Alone	27.50	37.50
	Total	**100.00**	**100.00**

PHYSICAL HEALTH

Health is basic to any discussion of the ageing experience, since health, particularly self-rating of health, is the most important determinant of satisfaction among the aged (Palmore and Clark, 1972). To simply state, that older people suffer more health problems is misleading but sure, their physical and mental health deteriorates, as they grow older. This work assessed various aspects of physical health of the respondents. The variables used for the measurement of the physical health of the aged include eye sight, hearing capacity, disability status, problems in physical movement, frequency of falling ill in a year, and effect of their overall physical health on activities of daily living (ADL).

Eye Sight

The eye sight of the older people seems not to be in good condition in both the villages. Respondents were asked to state the status of their eye sight. It is found that the eye sight level of more than half of the respondents from both the villages fail to be in good condition. Data in Table 3.9 reveals that the eyesight level of about 15 per cent of the respondents each in *Goila* and *Madwana*are very good. The respondents did not tell the specific reasons for poor eye sight, but few of them reportedly found suffering from cataract problem. Thus, the physical health of the elderly with related to their eye sight cannot be considered to be in good condition in both the villages which need to be intervened immediately.

Hearing Capacity

Regarding condition of hearing capacity, it is found that the hearing capacity of about 43 per cent in *Goila* and 50 per cent in *Madwana*are not in favourable condition. Table 3.9 shows that the hearing capacity of around 35 per cent of the respondents in *Goila* and 30 per cent in *Madwana* are good. Few elderly reported that they feel pain in their ears and because of this; they are not able to hear accurately.

Disability

The critical question concerning chronic conditions is the extent to which these conditions handicap the aged in their daily routines (Ward, 1979). Disability is an impairment that may be physical, cognitive, mental, sensory, emotional, developmental, or some combination of these. A disability may be present from birth, or occur during a person's lifetime. In the current study, some of the respondents are disabled. Table 3.9 shows that around 5 per cent of the respondents each in *Goila* and *Madwana* suffer from hearing and movement disability. The study also found that approximately 3 per cent of the respondents experience from speech and vision impairment in *Madwana*. Disability is the major constraint for disabled elderly in their daily routine of life.

Table 3.9: Physical Health of the Elderly

Sl.	*Level*	*Goila (%)*	*Madwana (%)*
1.	**Eye Sight**		
	Very good	15.00	15.00
	Good	30.00	32.50
	Not good	55.00	52.50
2.	**Hearing Capacity**		
	Very good	22.50	20.00
	Good	35.00	30.00
	Not good	42.50	50.00
3.	**Disability**		
	Seeing	0.00	2.50
	Hearing	5.00	5.00
	Speech	0.00	2.50
	Movement	5.00	5.00
4.	**Problem in Physical Movement**		
	Large extent	50.00	60.00
	Some extent	30.00	27.50
	Hardly any	20.00	12.50
5.	**Frequency of Falling Ill in a Year**		
	>2	30.00	22.50
	2 to 4	32.50	37.50
	<4	37.50	40.00
6.	**Effect of Physical Health on ADL**		
	Large extent	47.50	40.00
	Some extent	32.50	30.00
	Hardly any	20.00	30.00

Problem in Physical Movement

Half of the respondents experience problem in their physical movement to a large extent. Table 3.9 reveals that a considerable proportion of the respondents hardly face any problem with regard to their physical movements.

Frequency of Falling Ill

The frequency of falling ill of the respondents in a year was assessed.

Data in Table 3.9 shows that about 38 per cent of the respondents in *Goila* and 40 per cent in *Madwana* fall sick more than four times in a year. Study found that minimum 30 per cent of respondents in *Goila* and approximately 23 per cent in *Madwana* fall sick less than twice a year. Chronic diseases, with which they have been struggling with for a long time, are the main causes of falling sick more than four times in a year. The common chronic diseases found in the elderly are heart disease, cancer, arthritis, and diabetes, etc.

Effect of Physical Health on Activities of Daily Living (ADL)

Physical health and activities of daily living of the elderly are interrelated. Table 3.9 reveals that physical health problem affects about 48 per cent elderly in *Goila* and 40 per cent in *Madwana* to a large extent in their activities of daily living. They need help in their day-to-day work such as washing; clothing, bathing, and toilet, etc. There are around 20 per cent elderly in *Goila* and 30 per cent in *Madwana* who do not require any help for their ADL because they are physically well off.

MENTAL HEALTH

WHO describes mental health as "a state of well-being in which the individual realizes his or her own abilities, can cope with the normal stresses of life, can work productively and fruitfully, and is able to make a contribution to his or her community". Mental health assessment of the respondents was one of the essential aspects of the current study. Mental health of the respondents was assessed by using various variables such as ability to express the emotions, depression, death, fear, anxiety, sleeplessness, loneliness, forgetfulness, and effect of loss of dear ones.

Ability to Express the Emotions

Emotions are the conscious feeling of the elderly, which is associated with their mood, temperament, personality, and mental states.

Respondents were asked whether they are able to express their emotions with family members. A total of about 45 per cent of the respondents in *Goila* and 55 per cent in *Madwana* were hardly able to express their emotions with family members and about 35 per cent of the respondents in *Goila* and 25 per cent in *Madwana* were able to express their emotions to some extent while a significant proportion of the respondents were able to express their emotions to a large extent in both the villages.

Depression

Respondents were asked to state that to what extent they feel sad or depress. This study found that about half of the respondents feel depression to a large extent in both the villages and approximately 33 per cent of the respondents in *Goila* and 30 per cent in *Madwana* feel depression to some extent. There is significant proportion of the respondents in both villages who hardly feel depression. The study confirms that the familial problems are the main sources of depression among the respondents. The loss of their dear ones, poor economic and health condition, lack of support within the family, and family liabilities are the major factors, which affect the health condition of rural elderly.

Fear of Death

Attitude toward death are extremely complex and changeable, shifting with situation, mood, and cultural surroundings, and they vary by age, sex, education, religiosity, and so on. Death related attitudes are also very difficult to study, because of their sensitive emotional quality. The validity of responses to questions about death is also difficult to ascertain (Ward, 1979). The significant proportion of the respondents confessed that they have fear of death. About 45 per cent of the respondents in *Goila* and 48 per cent in *Madwana* have death fear to a large extent, which disturbs them mentally. It is also found that around 33 per cent of the respondents in *Goila* and 28 per cent in *Madwana* hardly face any death fear in their lives.

Table 3.10: Mental Health of the Elderly

Sl.	Level	Goila Percentage	Madwana Percentage
1.	**Ability to Express the Emotions**		
	Large extent	20.00	20.00
	Some extent	35.00	25.00
	Hardly any	45.00	55.00
2.	**Depression**		
	Large extent	47.50	57.50
	Some extent	32.50	30.00
	Hardly any	20.00	12.50
3	**Fear of Death**		
	Large extent	45.00	47.50
	Some extent	22.50	25.00
	Hardly any	32.50	27.50
4	**Sleeplessness**		
	Large extent	47.50	40.00
	Some extent	32.50	32.50
	Hardly any	20.00	27.50
5	**Loneliness**		
	Large extent	37.50	30.00
	Some extent	35.00	42.50
	Hardly any	27.50	27.50
6	**Forgetfulness**		
	Large extent	37.50	37.50
	Some extent	32.50	37.50
	Hardly any	30.00	25.00
7	**Effect of Loss of Dear Ones on Mental Health**		
	Large extent	50.00	57.50
	Some extent	30.00	32.50
	Hardly any	20.00	10.00

Sleeplessness

About 48 per cent of the respondents in *Goila* and 40 per cent in *Madwana* experience sleeplessness to a large extent. Data in Table 3.10 reveals that 20 per cent of the respondents in *Goila* and 28 per cent in *Madwana* hardly experience sleeplessness. Depression, social and financial liabilities, loss of dear ones, etc. also affects the sleeping pattern of the respondents.

Loneliness

Loneliness is a complex and usually unpleasant emotional response to isolation. It typically includes anxious feelings about lack of connectedness or communality with other beings, both in the present and extending into the future. As such, loneliness can be felt even when surrounded by other people. The causes of loneliness are varied such as social, mental, emotional, and spiritual factors. Loneliness is "Caused not by being alone but by being without some definite needed relationships" (Weiss, 1973). It is found that about 38 per cent of the respondents in *Goila* and 30 per cent in *Madwana* experience loneliness to a large extent. Around 28 per cent of the respondents in *Goila*or *Madwana* hardly experience loneliness in their lives.

Forgetfulness

As the elderly are being aged, their memory to remember and recognize, seems to be reduced, as reported by the respondents. The study found that approximately 38 per cent of the respondents in *Goila* and *Madwana* respectively experience forgetfulness to a large extent. Thirty per cent of the respondents in *Goila* and 25 per cent in *Madwana* have no problem with regard to their forgetfulness.

Effect of Loss of Dear Ones

The elderly have so much of concern in their life, which varies from personal to social but some respondents adapt themselves to their existing situation. The study found that loss of their dear ones affect hardly about 20 per cent of the respondents in *Goila* and 10 per cent in *Madwana*. Table 3.10 shows that more than half of the respondents are affected by loss of their dear ones to a large extent and they keep on thinking about them day and night even in their sub-conscious minds.

SUPPORT SYSTEM

Support system provides care to individual through social network. Support can come from many sources such as family, friends, organisations and co-workers. The support system for the elderly is required for their physical and mental care. Various support systems of the respondents were assessed. These are family, social and government. In addition, abuse of the elders and neglect were also assessed while focusing on the support systems of the elderly.

Family Support

The elderly, who are physically, mentally and financially frail, need support from the family members in their daily routine. Forty eight per cent of the respondents fail to receive good family support. In cases where the spouses are alive then they are taken care by the daughter in law and other members of the family. It is found that the attitudes of the daughter in laws towards their elderly are not very satisfying. However, Only 20 per cent in *Goila* and 28 per cent in *Madwana* receive very good family support, see Table 3.11.

Social Support

The support system is a kind of social network and society is one of the major stakeholders. The society also has certain responsibilities for their aged members. The elderly do not get the considerable social support from the society. Around 25 per cent of the respondents in the *Goila* and 20 per cent in *Madwana* receive a very good social support, see Table 3.12. At the same time, the study also found that more than half of the respondents do not receive good social support. This is despite the Indian rural communities well known for bearing characteristics such as bonding, togetherness, cohesiveness, and caring.

Table 3.11: Family Support for the Elderly

Sl.	Level	Goila (%)	Madwana (%)
1.	Very Good	20.00	27.50
2.	Good	32.50	25.00
3.	Not Good	47.50	47.50
	Total	**100.00**	**100.00**

Table 3.12: Social Support for the Elderly

Sl.	Level	Goila (%)	Madwana (%)
1.	Very Good	25.00	20.00
2.	Good	25.00	30.00
3.	Not Good	50.00	50.00
	Total	**100.00**	**100.00**

Government Support

It is observed that the government support for the elderly is very limited in both the villages. Only a few respondents could avail the government support in the form of old age pension. About 95 per cent of the respondents in *Goila* and 90 per cent in *Madwana* hardly receive any government support. There are various government provisions for the aged that can be facilitated by establishing a linkage between the government, *panchayat* and the beneficiary (aged). Social worker can play a crucial role as a mediator between these stakeholders for the advantage of the aged.

Elderly Abuse

The respondents face various forms of abuse pertaining to their identity, dignity, self-worth, physical inflict, injury, etc. In the current study, it was found that approximately half of the respondents experience elder abuse to a large extent in some form or other. Table 3.14 illustrates that about 23 per cent of the respondents in the *Goila* and 25 per cent in *Madwana* hardly experience abuse in their everyday life.

Table 3.13: Government Support for the Elderly

Sl.	*Level*	*Goila (%)*	*Madwana (%)*
1.	Large Extent	0.00	0.00
2.	Some Extent	5.00	10.00
3.	Hardly Any	95.00	90.00
	Total	**100.00**	**100.00**

Table 3.14: Elderly Abuse among the Respondents

Sl.	*Level*	*Goila (%)*	*Madwana (%)*
1.	Large Extent	47.50	50.00
2.	Some Extent	30.00	25.00
3.	Hardly Any	22.50	25.00
	Total	**100.00**	**100.00**

Neglect

This study also observed that the elderly face the problem of neglect in their lives. The study found that approximately half of the respondents experience neglect to a large extent in their lives. Table 3.15 shows that about 30 per cent of the respondents in the *Goila* and 23 per cent in *Madwana* experience neglect to some extent in their lives.

Table 3.15: Neglect of the Older People

Sl.	*Level*	*Goila (%)*	*Madwana (%)*
1.	Large Extent	45.00	57.50
2.	Some Extent	30.00	22.50
3.	Hardly Any	25.00	20.00
	Total	**100.00**	**100.00**

We examined the existing situation of the aged in the villages of *Goila* and *Madwana*. The next chapter presents the social work intervention strategies, processes, and influence in addressing the elderly issues.

4

Social Work Intervention

It is well documented that social work researchers work with people those who are vulnerable and struggle in some way to participate fully in society. Equally, it is well known that social work scholars provide interventions to individuals, families and groups in order to assist them with their needs and issues. Interventions are intended to aid clients in alleviating problems impeding their well-being. These interventions are those that are identified as potentially helpful on the basis of the researcher's ongoing assessment of the client (EHOW, 2014). A common vision for social work operating in complex human situations has been adopted. This is reflected in the following definition from International Association of Schools of Social Work and International Federation of Social Researchers: "the social work profession promotes social change, problem solving in human relationships and the empowerment and liberation of people to enhance well-being. Utilizing theories of human behaviour and social systems, social work intervenes at the points where people find difficulties in their social environment. Principle of human rights and social justice are fundamental to social work" (IFSW, 2014).

That said, it is reiterated that in the previous chapter, the existing situations of the elderly in experimental (*Madwana*) and control (*Goila*) village have been discussed. On the basis of the existing situations of the elderly with regard to their physical, mental health, and support system, social work intervention was introduced in *Madwana*. *Goila* was reserved as a control village to compare the effect of intervention. An intervention package consisting of various social work intervention strategies and procedures was designed to improve the conditions of aged in the experimental village. The present chapter intends to examine the social work intervention approach and procedure administered by the researcher in addressing the existing situation of the elderly.

Notwithstanding, every society has to solve problems in order to exist and survive in the physical and cultural environment. This requires the performance of a series of functions. How these universal functional problems are solved and how these requisite functions are performed is conditioned by the physical and cultural environment and by the passage of time, history, and traditions (Parsons, 1951, Davis, 1949, & Warren, 1963). Inherent in the existence of people and society is a dichotomous condition. Society must solve certain problems to ensure its continued existence and fulfill its needs or imperatives. People must also solve certain problems to ensure both their existence in social matrix and also the fulfillment of their own needs and strivings—which frequently are not in harmony with those of their society. A person's symbiotic relationship with the society and the variance of one's needs from those of society produces tensions, stresses, and strains. Abraham Maslow's hierarchy of needs postulates that higher types of human needs can only be gratified after lower types have been gratified. At the bottom, he places physiological and safety needs, moving upward to needs for love and belonging, further up to those for esteem, achievement, and recognition, then to self-actualization, and finally, to the needs to know and understand (Maslow, 1954).

When physiological, safety, and esteem needs have been reasonably well met, people are ready to find gratification in self-actualization and in understanding the world and their own existence in it; to take part in enjoying the gifts of life and nature; to enhance the quality of living for themselves and for their family, peers, and friends; to engage responsibly and creatively to improve the lives of others in their Faustian endeavour. We are, therefore, not only concerned with social functioning, but also with existential fulfillment. People today must learn to actualize themselves not only as members of their own culture and society, but also as members of a world society and a culture of all people. To assure people of all ages a minimum of security and the opportunity to function to the best of their ability and attain existential fulfillment as a participant in the world requires a number of social mechanisms and arrangements. Two major mechanisms by which society can develop a social security system designed to assure optimal existential conditions of all people are social policies and social practices (Lowy, 1979).

The tasks of social policy in many dynamic societies go beyond the present ones. Social policy should eventually become societal policy, which influences various societal functions in order to create conditions so that people can find creative fulfillment and self-realization as social participants. Social policy would indeed become the frame of reference, which guarantees not only existential social security but also existential fulfillment. The goal of such societal policy should be primarily directed toward changing the structures to make them more responsive to changing human needs at various stages of the life cycle within a societal context, and toward changing socio-cultural values and norms that are inimical to healthy growth and development, and therefore, inhibit full-range existential fulfillment through social participation for all ages. Such goals can be achieved through appropriate and knowledge interventive planning methods, which are predicated upon a problem solving approach (*ibid*).

Social problem solving originates in recognition on the part of an individual or a group that there is a disjunction between existing social situations (e.g. poor living condition of the aged) and an ideal state or standard. The recognition of a gap between present reality and some valued future state provides the impetus for initiating activities that are managed by an individual or a group who have been mandated or who have assumed the responsibility for planning (Perlman, 1970).

Social work is one field of practice that has carved out a domain for itself to deal with problems that people encounter with regard to their social functioning, and beyond that to enhance human fulfillment and self-realization through active social participation. It is one of the social practice mechanisms that intervene in order to mediate tensions between society's imperatives and a person's needs, desires, and expectations (Lowy, 1979).

The central goal of social work has been to enable people to improve their social functioning, that is, to carry out their social roles in a way that is consistent with their ego capacity (Boehm, 1959). A major focus has been on socially assisting people to cope with life situations and conditions, which present difficulties. Bartlett has taken this central idea and has elaborated it by stating that social work attempts to strike a balance between the demands of the social environment and people's coping efforts through working with them singly, in small groups, or in social organisations, either directly or through collaborative action. The following framework is used to delineate social work analytically as a field of practice on a continuum within a social matrix. The five components of social work practice with the elderly are values, purposes and goals, sanction, knowledge and the intervention repertoire (Bartlett, 1970).

VALUES

Social work is a normative profession and values have a significant impact on its practice. Values are defined as "conceptions of preferred and admirable things or characteristics of people" (Siporin, 1974) and preferred stances of thinking, feeling and doing." They affect the people toward whom practice is directed, as well as the quality of social work (Lowy, 1974). Two values have dominated the practice of social work: the worth, dignity and uniqueness of the individual and the right to self-determination by individuals, groups, or constituents in a community.

All practice is guided by values, or "preferred stances of behaviour". It may be more appropriate to speak of valuations rather than values since these imply an immutable universality that is based on "an objectivism that has no basis in logic and tends to concede much confusion" (Myrdal, 1968).

At least five categories of valuations have been identified: human nature, people's relationship to other people in society, society in relation to people, the process of knowing, and the process of helping. Under each category, a series of values can be subsumed on a high level of abstraction, which in turn must be operationalized beliefs crucible of practice. Conflicting valuations and inconsistent beliefs around in every society and in social work as well (Lowy, 1979).

PURPOSE AND GOALS

Three major purposes and goals of social work span the continuum from treatment to development: the curative and ameliorative, the preventive, and the promotional enhancing. The curative, treatment oriented goals have been accepted as a major province of social work. Intra and interpersonal tensions and stress conditions, role conflicts, deviant behaviour, and age-connected isolation of people have been traditional problem areas for social work intervention. Thoughts about public health and a raised public consciousness about social problems have moved social work towards prevention. These calls for attention to large scale social problems and commitment to action to deal with such persistent problems as poverty, drug, dependency, and alcoholism, and problems connected with the process of growing older and position of the elderly in society (*ibid*).

Commitment to the third goal, to promote and enhance the quality of life is of more recent origin. In the past, this goal was mostly expressed in the fields of recreation and informal and adult education rather than in the field of social work (Lowy, 1955). The developmental orientation, which now tends to become part of the goals and the practice of social work, especially in the developing countries of the world, seeks to create conditions for people that allow them to fulfill themselves optimally, find their place in tomorrow's world, and participate constructively and actively in the society as part of a large world. Fundamentally, this aspect of social work is oriented toward learning; it is the second and cultural part of the continuum (Lowy, 1979).

SANCTIONS

Social work, like any other field, is not practiced in a vacuum. It is given sanctions by the society, which extends its degree of legal authority for implementation of its purposes in a variety of services, agencies and by non-agency affiliated autonomous social researchers. When we view society as dynamic and ever changing, this accommodates conflicting forces and claims; when we view it as static and harmonious, this preserves a status quo (*ibid*).

KNOWLEDGE

Social work practice is based upon knowledge derived from a variety of disciplines: biology, psychology, sociology, social psychology, psychiatry, anthropology, law, theology, etc. It is also derived from the accumulated practice wisdom, or practice theory, that has emerged in the course of social work activities over the years. In addition, social welfare policies, programmes, and services represent a matrix of knowledge areas that are requisite for every social researcher. When we speak of knowledge, we need to differentiate between that which is definitely known, that which is tentatively known, that which is assumed to be known, and that which is yet unknown. Social work researcher practice is thus, predicted upon knowledge in varying states. If application by practitioners results in ready and efficient performance, we speak of such technical expertness as skills (*Ibid*).

THE INTERVENTION REPERTOIRE

Intervention is the "action of the practitioner which is directed to some part of the social system or social process with the intention of inducing a change in it" (Bartlett, 1970). Intervention aims at making a difference in outcome and in the course of events. It is guided by a constellation of values, purposes, and knowledge, and is based upon legal or institutional sanctions. It is justified on the basis of creative altruism.

Social work researcher has historically and declaratively shown regard for and devotion to, the interests of others through service. Creativity is a necessary condition for effective service to other people.

Intervention has historically involved methods of casework, group work, and community organisation. These methods have different historical roots and therefore, differ in development emphasis and focus. It is fundamental that each method contributes to a more inclusive and encompassing approach, which includes relevant knowledge and values as well as techniques. Interventive acts and techniques are means to an end and are only significant when the end is defined in terms of social work purposes and values and the situation is accurately understood with social work knowledge. It is through the conscious action of the social researcher, who selects what is relevant for the particular situation before him, that the appropriate knowledge and values become integrated with intervention (*ibid*).

This type of thinking has recently opened up a hitherto segmented practice orientation, which makes it possible to rearrange the knowledge and attendant methodological skills gained from casework, group work, and community organisation. New interventive repertories results, and the ingredients of the methods can be used for the widened purposes of social work and applied to the total purpose continuum. This includes treatment, when social functioning is impaired; action, to prevent problems that impinge on social functioning; and development, to enhance social functioning and allow for maximum self-realization for responsible and creative social participation. This is the realization of the responsible and creative social dimensions of human existence. There are five dimensions in the intervention repertoire: specific targets of intervention, specific goals for intervention, deduced from the more general purposes of social work, steps in the intervention process, activities of interveners, including modalities, methods, and techniques, and the roles of the intervener as enabler, broker, advocates, and expert (Lowy, 1979).

Therefore, the theoretical understanding of social work practice approach is the application of social work methods to the production of knowledge that social researchers need to solve problems they confront in the practice of social work. The knowledge is useful in appraising the effectiveness of the methods and techniques of social work. It provides information that can be taken into consideration by social researchers prior to making decisions that affect their clients, programmes or agencies such as use of alternative intervention techniques or change or modification of programme, and so forth. Social work practice offers an opportunity for all social researchers to make a difference or modification in the client's environment. There is no doubt about the fact that social research intervention will be more effective in addressing the client's problems by accomplishing the humanistic goals which start with problem identification and setting up of goals. This is followed by the process of assessment (or need assessment) of the clients problems. After the problem is identified and needs are assessed, the next step is to set up goals to be achieved. The goals are required to be specific, precisely defined and measurable in some way. The third step in the process is to have a pre-intervention measurement, that is, measurement prior to intervention. The pre-intervention measurement is used as a basis from which to compare the client's condition after the intervention has been introduced. Next stage in the process is to introduce intervention. In the last stage, assessment of the effects of intervention is made by comparing the two measurements, that is, pre-intervention measurement and measurements after intervention (Lal Das, 2010).

CONTEXT FOR SOCIAL WORK INTERVENTION

Situational analysis of the elderly during pre-intervention phase portraits the basis for social work intervention in *Madwana*. The baseline data showed that the respondents of *Madwana* have diverse socio-economic characteristics and less basic amenities. The research findings show that majority of the participants are illiterate with no occupation and therefore have no source of regular income. Most of the respondents fail to have access to drinking water and toilet facilities at their houses. Although the research unfolds that majority of the respondents are eligible to avail old age and widow pension but fails to have any access. The living condition and accommodation of the respondents are extremely diverse but of very poor quality. The food for most of the elderly are arranged by their spouses, relatives, and by themselves. Most of the respondents like to spend their leisure time with spouses, family members, and relatives.

The physical health including eye sight, hearing capacity and physical movement of the elderly are not good as reported by the respondents. Some of the elderly are disabled and fall sick more than four times a year due to various chronic diseases such as heart disease, cancer, arthritis, and diabetes, etc. In short, the research found that physical health problems affected most of the elderly in their activities of daily living. Majority of the elderly suffered from mental health problems such as depression, anxiety, sleeplessness, loneliness, and death fear. As the elderly is getting old, their memory to remember and recognize is getting reduced as reported by the respondents. Study found that loss of their dear ones affects about half of the respondents. Most of the elderly were not able to express their emotions with their family members. Existing family, social, and government support are not good for the most of the respondents. The respondents faced various forms of abuse and neglect.

Therefore, on the basis of issues emerged from baseline situation of the elderly in *Madwana,* social work intervention was implemented by the researcher to improve the condition of the elderly.

IMPLEMENTATION OF SOCIAL WORK INTERVENTION

The respondents are caught up with multiple problems with regard to their basic necessities, living arrangements, physical health, mental health, support system, elder abuse, and neglect. Subsequently comprehending these problems of the elderly, the researcher designed a set of strategic intervention goals to address these problems as shown in Table 4.1. The goals include improvement of the basic necessities of the elderly; to create better living conditions for them, to improve physical, mental health, and the support system, and to reduce elder abuse and neglect. The researcher had applied specific strategies, methods, values, and principles. The researcher played various roles while implementing social work intervention.

Table 4.1: Social Work Intervention Strategies

Areas of Intervention	*Intervention Goals*	*Intervention Strategies*
➢ Basic Necessities	To improve the basic necessities of the elderly	Networking, Advocacy, Awareness and Sensitization Programmes, Counselling, Focused Group Discussions, and Integrated Social Work Practice.
➢ Physical and Mental Health	To improve physical and mental health of the elderly	Active Ageing, Networking, Advocacy, Awareness, Sensitization, Recreational, and Motivational Programmes, Health Camps, Cognitive Therapy, Crisis Intervention Strategy, Counselling, Focused Group Discussions, Social Case Work, and Integrated Social Work Practice.
➢ Support System, Elder Abuse and Neglect	To improve the support system of the elderly and reduce elder abuse and neglect	Awareness and Sensitization Programmes, Counselling, Focused Group Discussions, and Integrated Social Work Practice.

INTERVENTION STRATEGIES APPLIED

Active Ageing

Active ageing is the process of optimizing opportunities for health, participation and security in order to enhance the quality of life as people age. It allows people to realize their potential for physical, social, and mental well-being throughout the life course and to participate in society, while providing them with adequate protection, security and care when they need (WHO, 2014). Several sessions were taken with the elderly and their family members especially children to make them understand about how elderly are important and can perform as a knowledge institution for individual and society. They were motivated to live happily and peacefully.

Advocacy

The researcher played a role of an advocate by advocating issues related to health, support system, and basic necessities of the elderly. The problems of the elderly were presented before competent authority by the researcher. The researcher assisted many respondents by visiting various offices such as community development block, health centres and *Panchayat Ghar* to raise the voices of the elderly.

Awareness, Motivational, Recreational, and Sensitization Programmes

The elderly respondents were having diverse problems and to prevent those problems several programmes such as awareness, motivational, recreational and sensitization were used. These programmes were implemented with the elderly, their family members, and society by using various techniques such as rally, counselling, group discussions, and recreational activities. These programmes provided opportunities for information gathering in order to improve understanding and develop competencies and skills necessary to enable changes in their situation.

Cognitive Therapy

Among the various therapy approaches, cognitive therapy had demonstrated significant effectiveness in the reduction of depression (Beck, Resnik, and Lettieri, 1974). The basic assumption underlying cognitive therapy is that dysfunctional cognition makes a person vulnerable to depression and lower self-esteem (Hammen, 1995). In the process, it was explained to the respondents that there were alternatives to their current problem producing behaviours. While addressing such dichotomous thinking and ineffective problem solving, the development of hope was facilitated. Most importantly, a sense of optimism was instilled into the respondents. The respondents were explicitly told that the 'feelings are not facts' and feeling hopeless did not mean that the situation was hopeless—it simply meant that you are feeling 'low' (Fremouw and others, 1990). The roles, the attitudes and beliefs played in creating their problematic emotions and behaviours, the degree to which they believed that they caused or controlled the events in their life were explained. It was helpful to demonstrate to the respondents that emotional state could be improved by changing how one processed experience. One of the many ways of demonstrating this point was to ask the respondents to think of examples of people coping well in difficult circumstances and to speculate how they managed to maintain their emotional well-being. This exercise almost always results in cognitive solutions, which can then provide ideas for use in the respondents' own life (Fremouw and others, 1990). Further, it was explained that if the respondents attributed failure to unstable factors like behaviour; it may not result in a deep and serious negative effect because there is still scope for success in the future. For instance, one may put in greater efforts and change one's style and behaviours leading to success (Parmeswaran and Beena, 2002).

Counselling

This technique was used at various stages while dealing with individual cases, interacting with children or family members of the elderly, and society. It is a personal help directed towards the solution of a problem, which a person finds that one cannot solve one's problem, and on which one, therefore, seeks the help of a skilled person whose knowledge, experience and general orientation can be brought into play in an attempt to solve the problem. Information and clarification are used for making the client aware of the problem in a psychological help. Counseling was very effective while dealing with health, family, social and personal issues of the respondents. Therapeutic counseling was used in intra-psychic conflict, mental health, and behaviour disorders. The purpose of such counseling was that of psychotherapy, which, aims at personality, competence and self-actualization, competence and self-actualization. For behaviour modification, researcher used techniques like positive enforcement and negative enforcement. Respondents were provided psychological support by counseling to decrease tension, anxiety, and loneliness.

Crisis Intervention Strategy

At the first instance, the crisis intervention approach (Golan, 1986) proved to be most urgent and effective in alleviating the emotional and mental turmoil associated with the elderly health. Social work counseling with specific sustainment techniques (Hollis and Woods, 1981) was designed to lower depression, guilt and tension and provided emotional support to the respondents. The relationship between the researcher and the client was of great importance. In order to elicit the needed information quickly and to inspire confidence that the researcher can help, a quick rapport, a state of understanding and comfort was developed between the client and the researcher (Golan, 1986). The researcher's attitude served as the controlling factor to facilitate an atmosphere that was non-threatening, genuinely warm, and realistically assuring. The researcher, throughout the intervention process, showed an attitude of interest. Facial expressions, tone of voice of words conveyed the researcher's genuineness. From time to time, the researcher felt the need to provide the respondents with opportunities to express his anxiety and gain relief through the process of ventilation (Hollis, 1972). The respondents gradually developed trust in the researcher's knowledge and goodwill. Likewise, the researcher expressed his confidence in the respondents' ability, recognized their capabilities and allowed them to feel freely to make decisions, thereby building their self-confidence. Subsequently, alternative ways of coping were explored to restore equilibrium (Coulshed and Orme, 1998). Help was given to sort out what worked and what did not work in the problem solving attempts.

Focus Group Discussions

Focus group discussions were held to improve physical, mental health and support system of the elderly by giving counseling sessions collectively. On few occasions the group was mixed with other family members, children, and the respondents.

Health Camps

Three health camps were organised with the help of local non-governmental organisation (NGO) namely Aarambh Welfare Foundation in the village. These health camps were common for all the villagers but the researcher gave a special emphasis on the elderly subjects and closely monitored, facilitated, assisted them. Two qualified doctors with their supportive team were engaged in the health camps. The local organisation was taken care by the *Gram Pradhan*. Hence, the researcher could use the technique of resource mobilisation while organizing a health camp. The health condition of the elderly such as eye sight, blood pressure, hearing capacity was assessed and necessary cases were referred to the nearest hospital. Besides, necessary medicines were distributed with the help of Aarambh Welfare Foundation.

Integrated Social Work Practice

Dealing with a variety of problems of the elderly integrated that social work practice was completely applicable as per the situation of the study. Social work methods, techniques, values, and principles were included together while working on health and living conditions of the aged.

Networking

Networking was used for fulfilling goals related to health and basic necessities such as old age pension, drinking water, and toilet facilities. Networking is basically a supportive system of sharing information and services among individuals and groups having a common interest. In this regard, the social work researcher established a cooperative and collaborative relationship with *Gram Pradhan*, Block Development Officer, Medical Officer at PHC, and *Block Pramukh* to address the issues of the elderly. The researcher met these officials several times.

Social Work Methods Applied

Social Case Work, Group Work, and Community Organisation methods are completely applicable and were followed by the researcher without any fail. Strengths based practice; home visits helped the researcher to obtain more information about their ability and strength. The researcher also conducted several sessions with the respondents, their children and other family members. Group discussions with the family and children too were very helpful to motivate them not to abuse and neglect the elderly.

Values Followed

Primary core values of social work, which were evident include dignity and worth of the person, importance of human relationship, competency, commitment, integrity, service, and responsibility. The researcher had introduced social researcher intervention wholeheartedly to help the elderly as a professional social work practitioner. The researcher showed the value of service while dealing with the respondents. Dignity and worth of the persons involved with every respondent was evident throughout the intervention process. The researcher had tactfully solved the complicated problem with his skills and capacities. The researcher's professional commitment and responsibility were seen throughout the process of the social work intervention. The value of responsibility was clearly evident in the study as the researcher could take up the entire intervention process in several months. Researcher showed respect for every relationship, which he made during the process of study and always proved his integrity.

Application of Social Work Principles

The researcher had carefully planned several strategies for intervention as well as applying various principles of social casework such as the principle of acceptance, client's right to self-determination, communication, individualization and confidentiality, etc. The application of the principle of acceptance was evident in the researcher's approach as he had accepted the situation and difficulties of the respondents and understood their strengths, limitations, potentialities, weaknesses, and misunderstanding. The researcher applied the principle of confidentiality in the study as promised to the respondents and to ensure professional commitment. The principle of communication had played crucial role in this case as the researcher could transmit the information according to the situation. This principle of controlled emotional involvement that was applied by the researcher was really needed in social work interventions particularly with individuals. In this study, the researcher had to apply the principle of controlled emotional involvement several times during the initial interaction with the respondents. The principle of non-judgmental attitude also played a crucial role, the researcher never judged the respondents' approaches and choices.

Specific Role played by the Researcher

The researcher had played specific roles while making social work intervention. As an enabler, the researcher assisted to the respondents to find the coping strengths and resources within themselves to produce the necessary change. As an advocate, the researcher became the voice for the respondents on various social and health issues and argued the elderly cause when this was necessary to accomplish. As a trained knowledgeable professional, the social researcher offered his skills, expertise, and body of knowledge in order to influence others in support of a social policy or to convince decision makers of the importance of particular programmes. Thus, the researcher played a role of an expert as well.

IMPACT OF SOCIAL WORK INTERVENTION

This section of the present chapter examines the impact of social work intervention and the comparability of experimental and control groups. There were no changes in the variables such as age, gender, marital status, religion, caste, educational status, occupations, and housing type as the similar sample of 80 elderly who were assessed at pre-intervention participated in post-intervention assessment. The living type and accommodation of the elderly remain unchanged in post-intervention assessment. There were few changes in the income level of the elderly in experimental village as about 7.5 per cent of the elderly started availing the government pension. Segment wise detailed post intervention assessment of the elderly have been presented below which examines the relevance of social work intervention in the area of the elderly care.

Basic Necessities

In order to improve the basic necessities of the elderly in *Madwana*, several intervention strategies were administered such as networking, advocacy, awareness, sensitisation programmes, counselling, focus group discussions, and integrated social work practice. The post intervention assessment revealed the differential impact of social work intervention on the basic necessities of the elderly in control and experimental village.

Drinking Water Facility

Pre and post data analysis revealed that before intervention, majority of the respondents were dependent on government hand pumps; whereas the dependency on government hand pumps has been reduced after social work intervention in *Madwana*. Chart 4.1 sketches that currently 48 per cent of the respondents have their own hand pumps, which

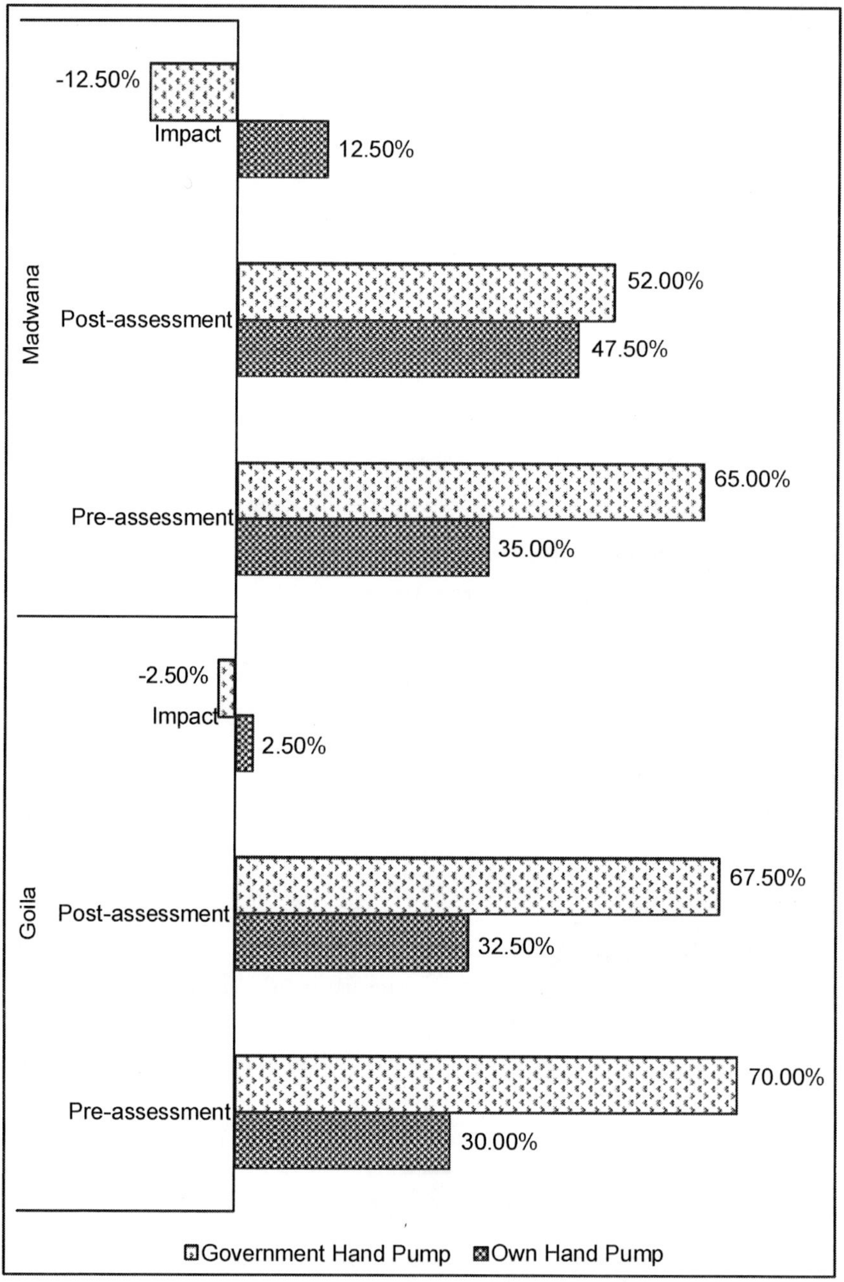

Chart 4.1: Impact of SWI on Drinking Water Facility

show the impact of interventions on 13 per cent of the elderly in *Madwana*. Post-intervention assessment found that one respondent in *Goila* had installed own hand pump with his own resources.

Toilet Facility

Pre-intervention assessment revealed that majority of the respondents had no accessibility to toilets in their homes. Chart 4.2 shows that after the intervention about 18 per cent of the respondents were motivated to construct toilets at their own houses with the support of their family members in *Madwana*, which results a significant impact of social work intervention as compared to control village where no improvement with regard to toilet facility was recorded during post-intervention assessment.

Government Pension

In spite of the eligibility for receiving old age and widow pensions, majority of the respondents could not avail the benefit of government pension scheme. Post-intervention data in Chart 4.3 unveils that about 8 per cent of the respondents were benefited by social work intervention for receiving the old age (5%) and widow (3%) pension in *Madwana* whereas no changes were found in *Goila.*

The food for the respondents are still arranged by their spouses, daughters in law and relatives in both the villages but the condition of the elderly who are alone has been improved in *Madwana* as compared to *Goila* as some of the respondents are being provided food by the family members. The respondents from both the villages spend their leisure time mostly with spouses, family members, relatives, friends, neighbours, and children. There are no major changes in both the villages with regard to their leisure time.

Physical and Mental Health

In order to improve the physical and mental health of the elderly in

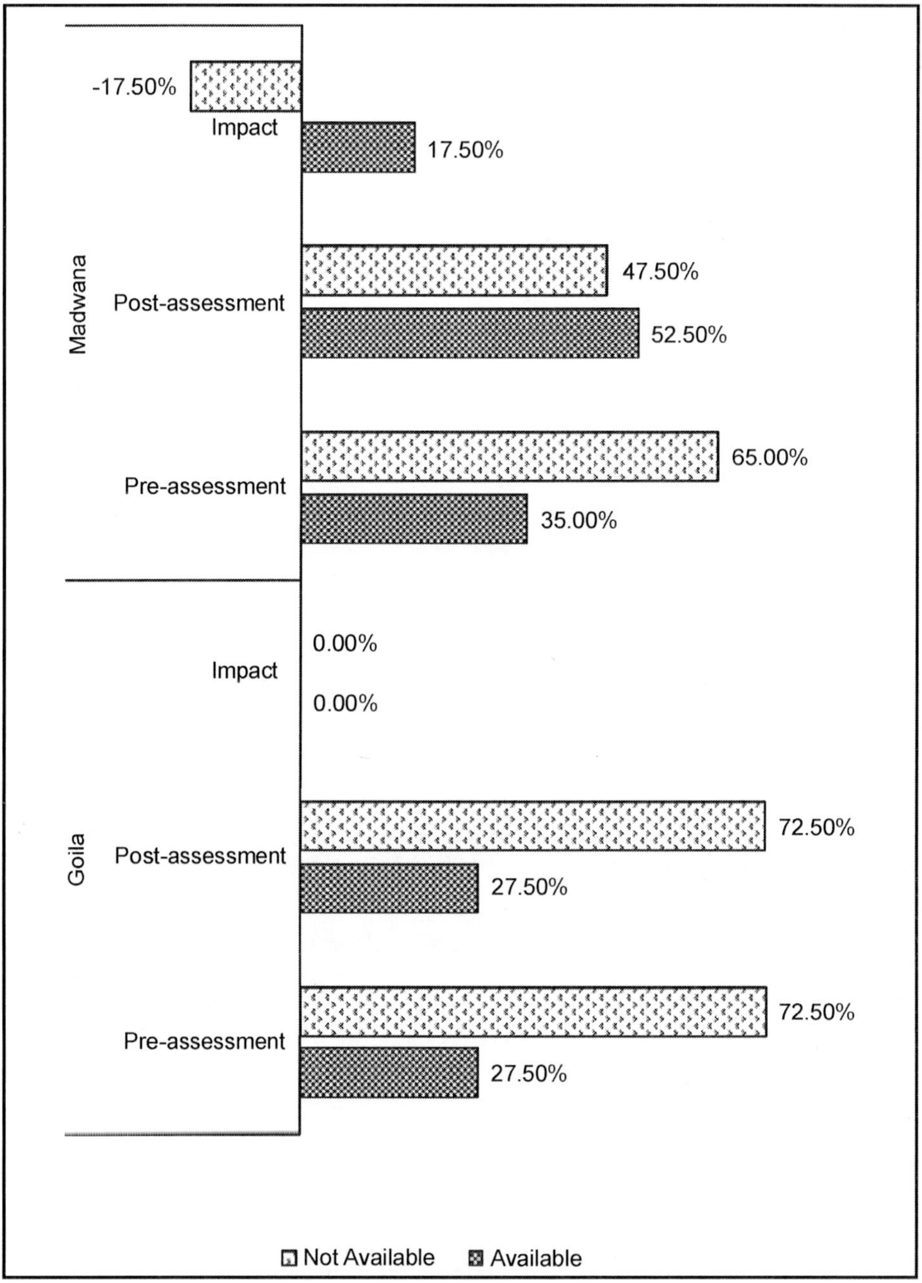

Chart 4.2: Impact of SWI on Toilet Facilty

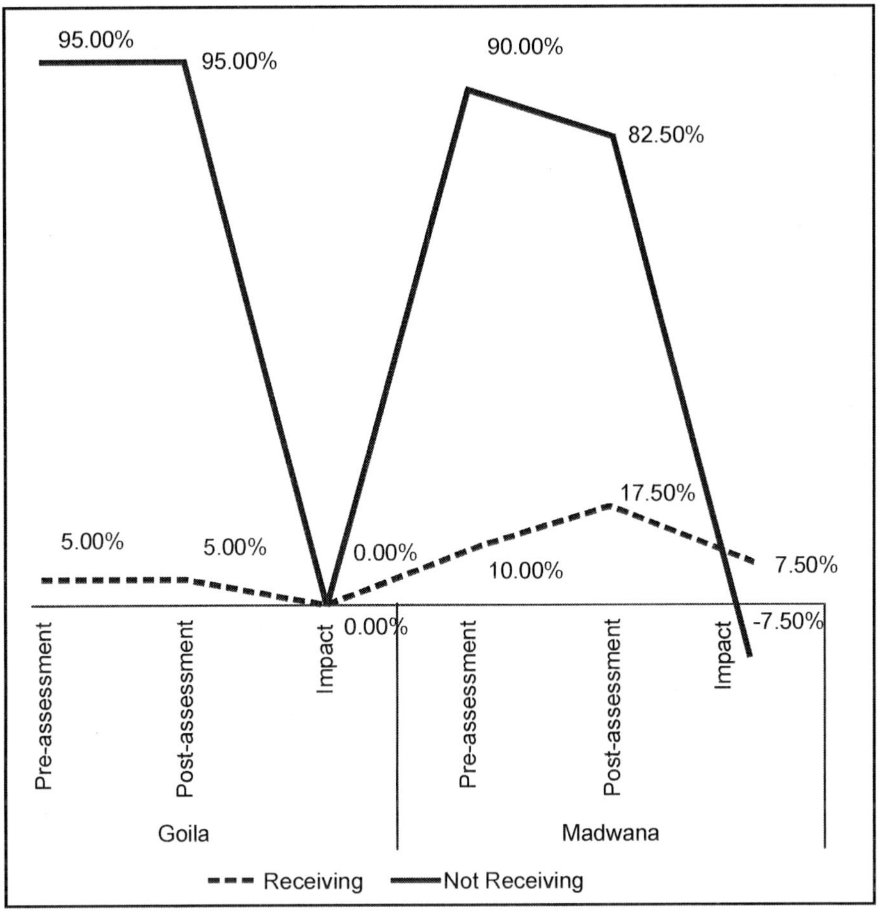

Chart 4.3: Impact of SWI on Government Pension

Madwana, several intervention strategies were administered such as active ageing, networking, advocacy, awareness, sensitisation, recreational, and motivational programmes, health camps, cognitive therapy, crisis intervention strategy, counselling, focus group discussions, social case work, and integrated social work practice. Various variables were used to determine the physical and mental health of the respondents. The post intervention assessment revealed the differential impact of social work intervention on the health condition of the elderly in both the control and experimental villages.

Eye Sight

The elderly were suffering from vision problem in both the villages. The specific reasons for low vision were not told by the respondents but few of them were found to be suffering from cataract problem. The eyesight of about 53 per cent of the respondents was not good during pre-intervention assessment in *Madwana.* Post-intervention data in Chart 4.4 reveals that after social work intervention 20 per cent of the respondents have been benefited. Two new cases of low vision were found during post-intervention assessment in *Goila*.

Hearing Capacity

Pre-intervention assessment found that the hearing capacity of about 43 per cent in *Goila* and 50 per cent in *Madwana* were not good. Post-intervention assessment shows that the hearing capacity of around 8 per cent of the respondents have been improved after social work intervention in *Madwana* with the support of hearing aids. Post-intervention data shows that about 5 per cent of the respondents were increased whose hearing capacity was not good in *Goila*.

Problem in Physical Movement

The pre-intervention study found that more than half of the respondents were experiencing problem in their physical movement to a large extent. Post-intervention assessment data in Chart 4.4 reveals that after social work intervention, the physical movement of 5 per cent of the respondents has been improved in *Madwana* whereas without intervention 3 per cent improvement was found in *Goila.*

Frequency of Falling Ill

The pre-intervention assessment showed that about 38 per cent of the respondents in *Goila* and 40 per cent in *Madwana* fall sick more than 4

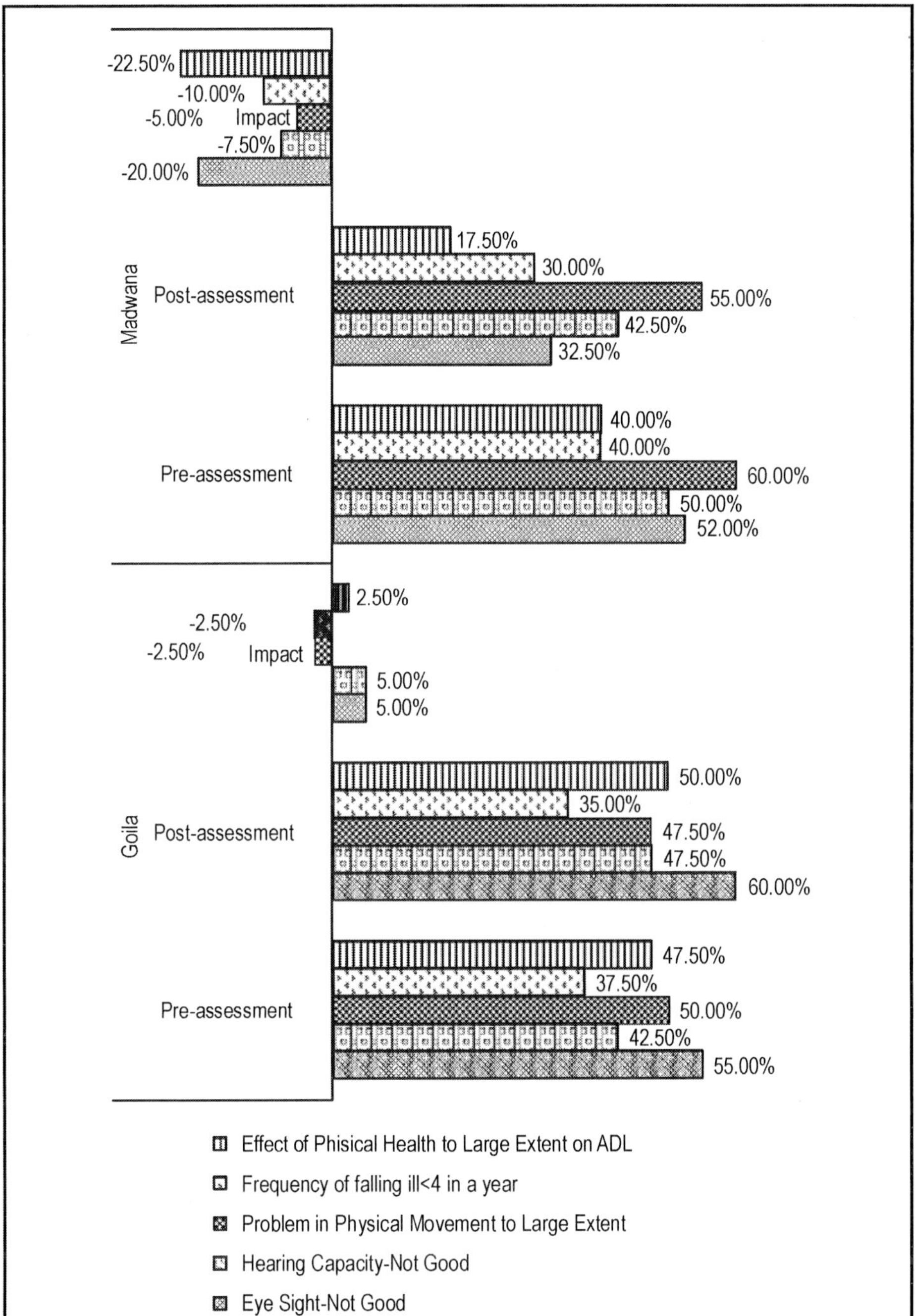

Chart 4.4: SWI and Physical Health of the Elderly

times in a year. Post-intervention assessment data in Chart 4.4 reveals that after social work intervention, the frequency of falling ill more than 4 times in a year was reduced in the *Madwana* up to 10 per cent whereas 3 per cent improvement was found in *Goila*. The significant impact of social work intervention has been examined in frequency of falling ill.

Effect of Physical Health on ADL

In the pre-intervention study, it was found that physical health problem affects about 48 per cent the elderly in *Goila* and 40 per cent in *Madwana* to a large extent in their activities of daily living. Post-intervention assessment found that after social work intervention the effect of physical health to large extent on their activities of daily living has been reduced on 23 per cent of the respondents in *Madwana*. The effect of physical health largely on ADL has been increased to 3 per cent of the respondents during post-intervention study in *Goila*.

Ability to Express the Emotions

In pre-intervention assessment, about 45 per cent of the respondents in *Goila* and 55 per cent in *Madwana* were hardly able to express their emotions with their family members. Post-intervention data in Chart 4.5 reveals that social work intervention has improved the ability to express the emotions of 10 per cent elderly in *Madwana* whereas the ability to express the emotions of the elderly has not improved in *Goila* and 3 per cent the elderly were increased who were not able to express their emotions with their family members during pre intervention.

Depression

Pre-intervention assessment found that more than half of the respondents were experiencing depression to a large extent in *Madwana* whereas post-intervention assessment reveals that the depression to a large extent

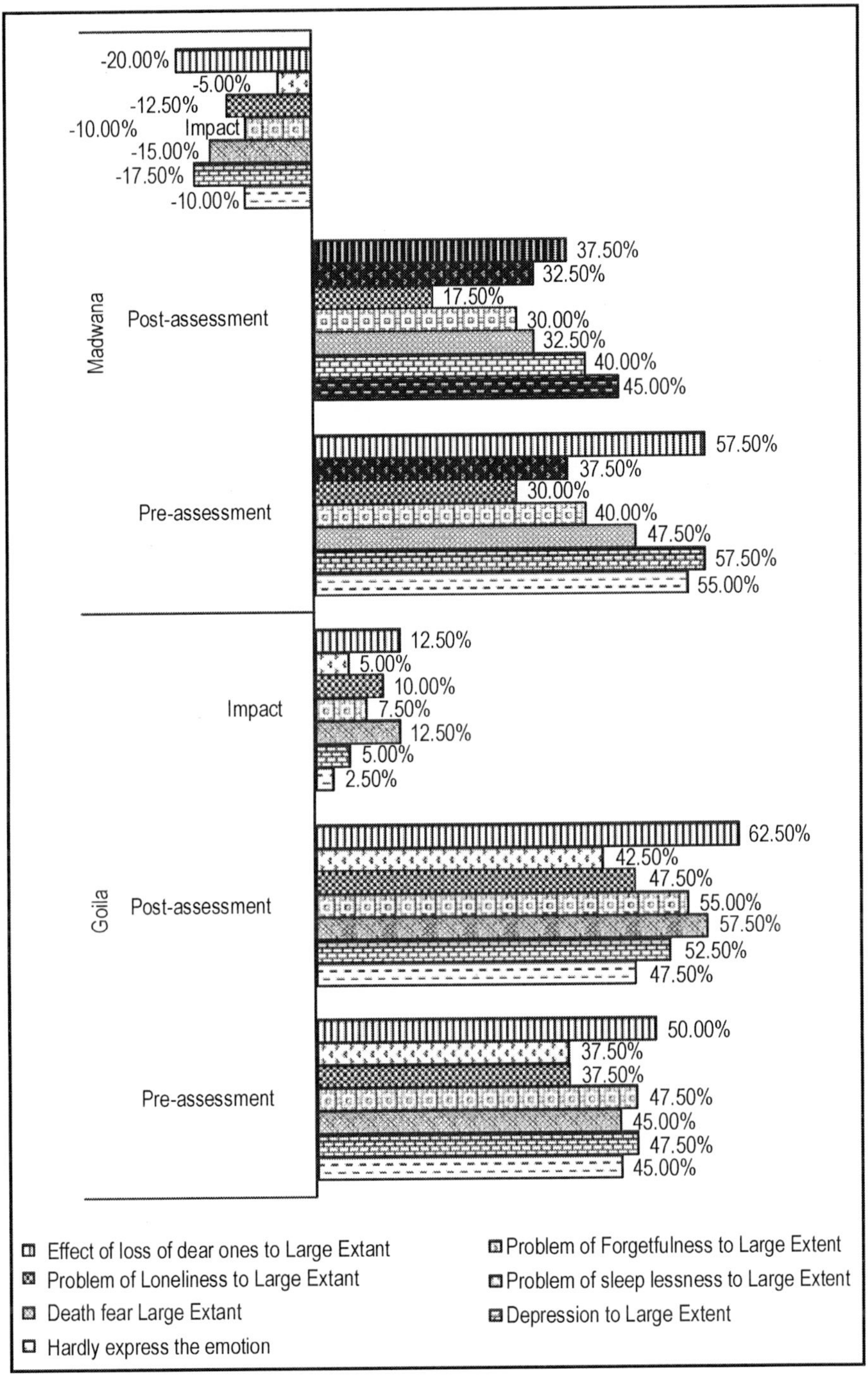

Chart 4.5: SWI and Mental Health of the Elderly

has been reduced after social work intervention and about 15 per cent of the respondents have been benefited from the intervention. Data in Chart 4.5 shows the improvement in depression to a large extent on about 5 per cent of the respondents in *Goila*.

Death Fear

Pre-intervention data shows that about 45 per cent of the respondents in *Goila* and 48 per cent in *Madwana* suffered from the fear of death. Post-intervention assessment found that after social work intervention the fear of death has been reduced in 15 per cent of the respondents in *Madwana*. Data in Chart 4.5 reveals that the fear of death to a large extent has been increased in 13 per cent of the respondents in *Goila*.

Sleeplessness

Pre-intervention study found that about 48 per cent of the respondents in *Goila* and 40 per cent in *Madwana* experience sleeplessness to a large extent. Post-intervention assessment found that after social work intervention the problem of sleeplessness to a large extent has been reduced in 10 per cent of the respondents in *Madwana*. Data in Chart 4.5 reveals that the problem of sleeplessness to large extent has been increased in 8 per cent of the respondents in *Goila*.

Loneliness

In the pre-intervention study, it was found that about 38 per cent of the respondents in *Goila* and 30 per cent in *Madwana* were experiencing loneliness to large extent. Post-intervention assessment found that after social work intervention the problem of loneliness to a large extent has been reduced in 13 per cent of the respondents in *Madwana*. Data in Chart 4.5 reveals that the problem of loneliness to a large extent has been increased in 10 per cent of the respondents in *Goila*.

Forgetfulness

Pre-intervention study found that about 38 per cent of the respondents in *Goila* and *Madwana* were experiencing forgetfulness to a large extent respectively. Post-intervention assessment found that after social work intervention the problem of forgetfulness to a large extent has been reduced in 5 per cent of the respondents in *Madwana*. Data in Chart 4.5 reveals that the problem of forgetfulness to a large extent has been increased in 5 per cent of the respondents in *Goila*.

Effect of Loss of Dear Ones

Pre-intervention study found that the loss of dear ones affect more than half of the respondents to a large extent in both the villages. Post-intervention assessment found that after social work intervention the effect of loss of dear ones to large extent has been reduced in 20 per cent of the respondents in *Madwana,* which shows a significant impact of social work intervention. Data in Chart 4.5 reveals that the effect of loss of dear ones to a large extent has been increased in 13 per cent of the respondents in *Goila*.

Support System, Elder Abuse and Neglect

For improving the support system of the elderly and reduce elder abuse and neglect several intervention strategies were administered in *Madwana*. The intervention strategies include awareness and sensitisation programmes, counselling, focus group discussions, and integrated social work practice.

Family Support

Pre-intervention study found that about 48 per cent of the respondents in *Goila* and *Madwana* were not receiving good family support. Post-intervention assessment found that after social work intervention about

25 per cent of the respondents have been benefited in *Madwana*, which shows a significant impact of social work intervention. Post-intervention data in Chart 4.6 reveals that about 5 per cent of the respondents have been increased who do not receive good family support in *Goila*.

Social Support

Pre-intervention assessment showed that around 50 per cent of the respondents in the *Goila* and *Madwana* were not receiving good social support. Post-intervention assessment found that after social work intervention about 13 per cent of the respondents has been benefited who were not receiving good social support in *Madwana*. Post-intervention data in Chart 4.6 reveals that about 8 per cent of the respondents have been increased who do not receive good social support in *Goila*.

Government Support

Pre-intervention study revealed that about 95 per cent of the respondents in *Goila* and 90 per cent in *Madwana* hardly receive any government support. Post-intervention assessment found that after social work intervention about 15 per cent of the respondents has been benefited who hardly receiving government support in Madwana were. Post-intervention data in Chart 4.6 reveals that no respondent has been benefited for government support in *Goila* in the period of last six months.

Elder Abuse

Pre-intervention study showed that about 48 per cent of the respondents in *Goila* and 50 per cent in *Madwana* were experiencing elder abuse to a large extent in their day to day life. Post-intervention assessment found that after social work intervention, the elder abuse to a large extent has been reduced in 18 per cent of the respondents in *Madwana*, which

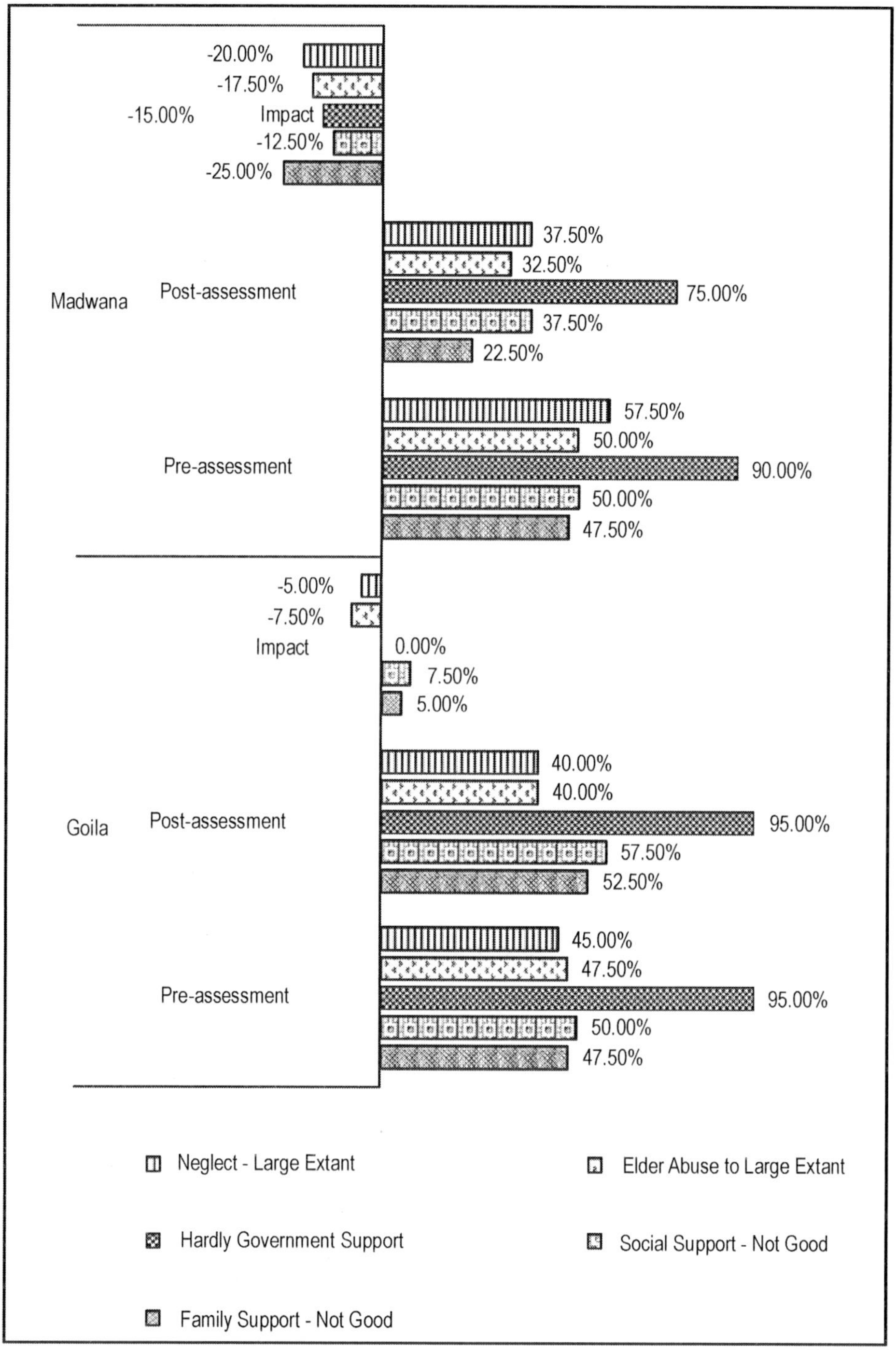

Chart 4.6: Impact of SWI on Support System, Elder Abuse, and Neglect

shows a significant impact of social work intervention. Data in Chart 4.6 reveals that the elder abuse to a large extent has also been reduced in 8 per cent of the respondents in *Goila*.

Neglect

Pre-intervention data revealed that about 45 per cent of the respondents in *Goila* and 58 per cent in *Madwana* experience neglect to a large extent in their life. Post-intervention assessment found that after social work intervention, neglect of older people reduced greatly in 20 per cent of the respondents in *Madwana.* This obviously shows an important impact of social work intervention. Data in Chart 4.6 reveals that neglect of older people to a large extent has been reduced in 5 per cent of the respondents in *Goila* as well.

In sum, here we examined the social work intervention and its impact in the care of the aged. The next chapter presents the six in-depth case studies, where intensive social work intervention has been dealt.

5

Learning from Individual Case Studies

This chapter delves deep on six individual case studies, which are both sensitive and important. All these six case studies were conducted in the *Madwana* village. Individual casework focuses on the person and his/her social environment and helps to advance the balance between the coping efforts and the social environmental demands of the person. Social caseworker provides help to the individuals to cope more effectively with their problems in social functioning through this method. Accordingly, the process of social casework as propounded by Mary Richmond in 1917 has been followed. This method calls for social investigation or psycho-social study, diagnosis, and treatment. In order to retrieve information using social casework as intervention strategies, rapport was established by the author with the clients and followed the principle of individualization by accepting them as unique persons in a stressful position. In order to administer the phases of casework, author conducted various sessions with each client. During fieldwork, he also recorded all the cases that were dealt with. Therefore, this chapter presents six case studies, which illustrates in-depth understanding about the condition of the elderly in rural areas. In addition, it provides how the problems of elderly at individual level can be addressed by using social work methods, values, and principles.

CASE STUDIES

Case of Chaurana

Personal Background

Chaurana, a 64-year old widow resides in a joint family with her children in the village *Madwana*. She belongs to upper caste ordinary *Hindu* family. Although, she was deprived of having any formal education from any institution but she possesses good understanding about human behaviour. Her husband died five years ago. He was suffering from cancer. He was a government primary school teacher and the sole breadwinner of his family. Chaurana has five children including one daughter and four sons. Her daughter and eldest son are married and other three sons are yet to marry. Modest basic facilities such as drinking water and toilet are available at her house. Her house is *pucca* (cemented and permanent). Chaurana receives government pension after the death of her husband. This is her only source of income.

Problem Assessed

In the process of assessment of the problem, the worker tried to secure each and every minute detail of Chaurana in order to reveal her personality and the situation for appropriate intervention. It was the initial phase in which the worker gained his first understanding about the need of Chaurana. After establishing a strong rapport with Chaurana, the worker studied the case thoroughly by doing home visits and conducted several sessions for identifying her existing problems. Subsequently after several visits and detailed discussions with Chaurana, the worker understood the actual problems—her key problems are passing away of her husband five years ago; none of her children were married nor settled at the time of her husband's death. Therefore, she was burdened with many liabilities such as children's marriage; their settlement. Somehow, she could able to manage her two children's marriage. In addition to these problems, she also reported that she faced enormous sufferings in her married life—indeed was a victim of domestic violence. Neither her husband nor her other family members showed any love and affection towards her. Although her husband was a primary school teacher, he was an alcohol addict. As a result of alcohol addiction of her husband, she was beaten many a times. Taking advantage of her abusive husband, other family members such as mother-in-law and sister in laws also abused her. In fact, in her married life she did not receive any respect from her husband and other family members of her in-laws. She was not given even a single rupee for her immediate needs. Her husband used to keep his monthly salary with his sister. Chaurana shared that she was alive with the hope that one day everything would be all right once her children grow. Nevertheless, she did not receive any respect from her two sons. Her youngest son love and respect her but he lives in a city for his studies and often visit her. Currently, she is able to have some form of financial support only because of her husband's pension. Although, her husband did not support her financially, socially and psychologically, however, pension is the only support, which her husband left for her after his death. The client was caught up with multiple existing problems such as abuse, neglect, lack of family support, sleeplessness, loneliness, stress, and other liabilities such as children's marriage and their settlement. Due to these problems, her memory has been reduced. The worker decided to help the client from her existing problems through the help of social work intervention.

Social Work Intervention

After comprehending the case in detail, the caseworker designed a set of intervention goals to address the problem. The goals include: sensitize family members on various aspects, create better support system among the family members and her children, motivation and encouragement to face the existing situation. The worker had formulated strategic goals to address Chaurana's problem. The worker had applied specific strategies such as counselling, sensitisation and motivational programmes including conducting as many as sessions to know more details about the case in a professional way to resolve the issues. The worker took several sessions with Chaurana over a period of six months and visited to the client's home on various times, which built rapport and trust on them, which in turn helped the worker to make a successful intervention.

Methods and Techniques Applied

Social Case Work method was completely applicable in this case and the worker without any fail followed that. Home visits helped the worker to obtain more information. He could get clarity on the issue and initiate the interaction with the client. The worker also conducted several interviews with Chaurana, her children and other family members. To encourage the strength of Chaurana, strengths based practice method was administered as well. Group discussions with the family and children too were helpful to motivate them not to abuse and neglect Chaurana.

Values Followed

Primary core values of social work, which were evident in the case, include dignity and worth of the person, importance of human relationship, competency, commitment, integrity, service, and responsibility. The worker had taken the case wholeheartedly to help the client as a professional social work practitioner. The worker showed the value of service while dealing with the client. Dignity and worth of the persons involved in the case was evident throughout the intervention process. The worker had tactfully solved the complicated problem with his skills and capacities. The worker's professional commitment and responsibility were seen throughout the process of the case. The value of responsibility was clearly evident in this casework as the worker could take up the entire casework process in several months. Worker showed respect for every relationship, which he made during the process of casework and always proved his integrity.

Application of Social Work Principles

The worker had carefully planned several strategies for intervention as well as applying various principles of social casework such as the principle of acceptance, client's right to self-determination, communication, individualization and confidentiality, etc. The application of the principle of acceptance was evident in the worker's approach as he had accepted the situation and difficulties of the client and understood the client's strengths, limitations, potentialities, weaknesses, and misunderstanding. The worker applied the principle of confidentiality in this case as promised to the client and ensured professional commitment. The principle of communication had played crucial role in this case as the worker could transmit the information according to the situation while the client narrated the problems and took pauses several times. During that time, the response of the worker in a positive way with emphatic nature plays a vital role. If there is miscommunication during such situations, the client may not be able to cope up with her emotions. The principle of controlled emotional involvement that was applied by the worker was really needed in social work interventions particularly with individuals. In this case, the worker had to apply the principle of controlled emotional involvement several times during the initial interaction with the client. The principle of non-judgmental attitude played a crucial role, the worker never judged the client's approaches and choices.

Evaluation

It was a difficult case in terms of nature of problem, associated with several aspects. The worker had tactfully dealt with the case by applying suitable strategies in every context. Otherwise, it would have been a very difficult to reach the goals of the case. By applying various methods, following certain principles, the worker could address the multiple problems in the same case with his extraordinary skills and humanity qualities apart from following the principles, values of social work at every step. Currently, Chaurana's unmarried children and other family members have started showing respect to her. Her three sons care for her health and other necessities. Chaurana is happy to receive the care and support from her three sons and family members. She had now arranged her two son's marriage. However, her eldest son's behaviour towards her has not changed. Overall, she experiences better days at the edge of her life and lives happily with her children and other family members without much worry.

Case of Ashok

Personal Background

Ashok, a 69-year old man was born in a schedule caste ordinary *Hindu* family. He resides in the *Madwana* village with his spouse and four unmarried children. He did not attain any formal education. He is a daily wage labourer and economically deprived. His married son lives in a separate family while married daughter stays at her husband's house. Ashok has two brothers who reside in the same village. His house is semi *pucca* (half cemented) with no toilet and drinking water facility at his house.

Problem Assessed

The worker studied the case thoroughly via regular home visits and conducted several sessions in order to identify his existing problems. Problem assessment is a systematic study of the client's circumstances where the worker tries to retrieve each and every detail about the client that reveals the client's personality and the situation for appropriate intervention. After rigorous community visits, the worker established a strong rapport with Ashok. After several visits and detailed discussions with the Ashok, the worker understood the actual problems. The health condition of the Ashok is poor. He suffers from tuberculosis and therefore, most of the time he remains sick. As a consequence of this,

Ashok is facing a huge financial crisis. Except for this wife, neither his sons nor his family members support him for his poor health. His wife is also old and is not able to help him appropriately. Therefore, Ashok primarily facing two types of problems, which include immediate and long term. Immediate problems consist of lack of financial support, treatment for tuberculosis, and stress. Long-term problems include lack of family support, disrespect from children, denial, and abuse, etc. The worker decided to help the client from his existing problems by using social work methods, techniques, principles, and values. The assessment phases gave realistic basis about the client's social environment.

Social Work Intervention

The objective of social work intervention is to alleviate the client's distress while restoring, maintaining or enhancing the social functioning of the client. After understanding the case of Ashok in detail, the caseworker designed a set of intervention goals to address both the immediate and long term problems of Ashok by formulating strategic goals to address his problem. The worker had applied specific strategies including conducting as many sessions as possible to gather more details about the case in a professional way and to resolve these issues. To intervene in his immediate problems, the worker decided to assist him to obtain his old age pension with the help of the local head of the *Panchayat* (*Pradhan*) and to facilitate him in his physical health (tuberculosis); the worker then tried to build linkage between Ashok and the Primary Health Centre (PHC) with the support of their sons and family members. To interfere in his long-term problems, worker took various sensitisation sessions with Ashok's sons and family members. The worker's visits to the Ashok's home several times had helped in the intervention process

Methods and Techniques Applied

Diverse methods and techniques were used in the process of social work intervention. Social Casework method was completely applicable in this case and the worker without any fail followed that. Home visits helped the worker to obtain detailed information. He could get clarity on the issue and initiate the interaction with Ashok. The worker also conducted several interviews with Ashok, his children and other family members. To encourage the strength of the client, strengths based practice method was administered as well. The worker played a vital role as advocate, mediator and expert while linking the client to receive old age pension and treatment for physical health at PHC. The worker also played a role of an enabler and mentor while taking several sessions and dealing with the client's long-term problems.

Values Followed

The worker had followed various social work values while dealing with the client. Major core values of social work, which were evident in the case of Ashok, include competency, service, dignity and worth of the person, integrity, importance of human relationship, commitment, and responsibility. Dignity and worth of the persons involved in the case was evident throughout the intervention process. By using the value of competence, the worker had tactfully solved the complicated problems with his skills and capacities; the worker's professional commitment and his responsibility were seen throughout the process of the case, the worker had taken the case sincerely to help Ashok as a professional social work practitioner and applied the value of social work service. The value of integrity was clearly evident in this case work as the worker could take up the entire casework process without compromising Ashok's and his integrity. The worker maintained human relationship with every person during the entire casework process.

Application of Social Work Principles

The worker had meticulously planned several strategies for intervention as well as applying various principles of social casework such as the principle of acceptance, confidentiality, individualization, evaluation, communication, client's right to self-determination, etc. The worker applied the principle of confidentiality in the case of Ashok and as promised, the worker ensured professional commitment. The principle of communication had played a crucial role in this case of Ashok and the worker could transmit the information according to the situation while the client narrated the problems. During such time, the response of the worker in a positive way and emphatic nature plays a vital role. If there is miscommunication during such situations, the client may not be in a position to cope with his emotions. This principle helped while referring Ashok to the PHC. The application of the principle of acceptance was evident in the worker's approach as he had accepted the situation and difficulties of Ashok and understood his strengths, limitations, potentialities, weaknesses, and misunderstanding. The principle of controlled emotional involvement that was applied by the worker was really needed in social work interventions particularly with individuals. The principle of non-judgmental attitude played a crucial role, the worker never judged the client's approaches and choices. In this case, the worker had to apply the principle of controlled emotional involvement several times during the initial interaction with client.

Evaluation

The worker had dealt with the case by applying suitable strategies in every context. It was a difficult case in terms of the nature of problem, associated with several aspects. By applying various methods and techniques, following certain values and principles, the worker could address the multiple problems in the same case with his extraordinary skills and humanity qualities apart from following the principles, values of social work at every step. As a consequence of intervention, Ashok's name for old age pension has been included in the list of beneficiary. However, there was no follow-ups made but it has been assumed that probably Ashok is receiving his old age pension right now. However, Ashok started receiving the treatment free of cost for tuberculosis from which he has been suffering. For the long-term problems, the worker took various sessions with the family members and with the children of Ashok. He reported that currently he did not face any abuse neither from his family members nor from his sons. Thus, the social work intervention could improve the quality of life of the client.

Case of Ramasare

Personal Background

Ramasare, a 74-year old man resides in the *Madwana* village with his two married children. He was born in the family belonging to the other backward community (OBC). He has lost his wife two years ago. He accomplished his education up to fifth standard from the local primary school and worked as a helper in a factory in the Lucknow city. He has an average economic support; both of his sons work in a private sector in the city. His family consists of nine members including two sons, two daughters-in-law, three grandsons and a granddaughter. Ramasare has four brothers and two of them reside in the same village. His house is semi *pucca* (half cemented). He has no access to toilet and drinking water facilities at his house.

Problem Assessed

Problem assessment is the initial phase in which the worker gained his first understanding about Ramasare's needs. After various community visits and sessions, the worker established a strong rapport with Ramasare. The worker studied the case thoroughly and understood the actual problems. Ramasare was caught up with multiple existing problems: lack of support system, poor physical, and mental health. The client was suffering from various physical health problems such as low eye sight, problem in physical movement, and poor hearing capacity. As a consequence of his poor health condition, Ramasare fails to receive good family support. The worker was surprised to learn that a 74-year-old man in a patriarchal society like India prepares and cooks his own food. The worker decided to help the client from his existing problems.

Social Work Intervention

The worker designed a set of intervention strategies to alleviate the Ramasare's existing conditions. He took up all the problems of Ramasare one by one. He referred Ramasare to the nearest PHC for his physical health problems. The worker facilitated entire process such as reaching the PHC and introducing Ramasare to the doctor. The worker also carried out various counselling sessions with the sons and daughter in laws of Ramasare for not to behave roughly with him. Following this, the worker took personal sessions with Ramasare to enhance his coping mechanism to reduce his mental stress and worries. With his strategic goals, the worker could address Ramasare's problems one by one. The worker had applied specific strategies including conducting as many counseling sessions he could to resolve the issues. The worker then visited Ramasare's home several times for the purpose of successful social work intervention.

Methods and Techniques Applied

Various methods and techniques were used during the entire process of social work intervention. Social Casework method was completely applicable in this case and the worker without any fail followed that. Home visit helped the worker to obtain more information. He could get clarity on the issue and initiate the interaction with Ramasare. The worker also conducted several counseling sessions with Ramasare, his sons and other family members. To enhance the strength and coping mechanism of Ramasare, strengths based practice and resilient social work methods were administered as well.

Values Followed

Primary core values of social work, which are evident in the case, include service, commitment, and responsibility, competency, integrity, dignity and worth of the person, and importance of human relationship. Service is a major value and the worker had followed it sincerely to help the Ramasare as a professional social work practitioner. The worker's professional commitment and responsibility were seen throughout the process of the case. The worker showed his competence and had tactfully solved the complicated problem with his skills and capacities. The value of integrity was clearly evident in this case work as the worker could take up the entire case work processes in several months without compromising Ramasare's and his integrity. Dignity and worth of the persons involved in the case was evident throughout the intervention process.

Application of Social Work Principles

The worker had used various social work principles and had meticulously planned several strategies for intervention. The principles applied during the social work intervention comprise the principle of acceptance, confidentiality, individualization, evaluation, communication, client's right to self-determination, etc. The application of the principle of acceptance was evident in the worker's approach as he had accepted the situation and difficulties of Ramasare and understood his strengths, limitations, potentialities, weaknesses, and misunderstanding. The worker applied the principle of confidentiality and ensured professional commitment. The principle of communication had played crucial role in this case as the worker could transmit the information according to the situation while Ramasare narrated the problems. The principle of communication helped during the referral service for Ramasare to the PHC. The principle of controlled emotional involvement that was applied by the worker was really needed in social work interventions particularly with individuals. In this case, the worker had to apply the principle of controlled emotional involvement several times during the initial interaction with Ramasare. The principle of non-judgmental attitude played a crucial role, the worker never judged the client's approaches and choices.

Evaluation

It was a difficult case in terms of nature of the problem, associated with several aspects. By applying various methods, following certain principles and values, the worker could address the problems of Ramasare with his extraordinary skills and humanity qualities apart from following the principles, values of social work at every step. Currently, there is improvement in the physical and mental health condition of the client. After the intervention, the daughters-in-law of Ramasare cook food for him on the basis of a standard rotation. Therefore, the social work intervention has changed the existing situation of Ramasare by bringing in family support system and improved health condition through his access to PHC.

Case of Devki

Personal Background

Devki, a 67-year-old woman resides in the village *Madwana* with her spouse and married children. She belongs to the schedule caste (SC) community. She completed her education till the third standard. Modest basic facilities such as drinking water and toilet are available at her house. Her house is semi *pucca* (half cemented). She has no source of income and is dependent on her sons.

Problem Assessed

In the process of assessment of the problems, the worker tried to obtain each and every detail of Devki that revealed her personality and the situation for appropriate intervention. It was the initial phase in which the worker gained his first understanding about the need of Devki. After establishing a strong rapport with Devki, the worker studied the case thoroughly by doing home visits and conducted several sessions for identifying her existing problems. After subsequent visits and detailed discussions with Devki, the worker understood the actual problems. She was not caught up with multiple problems. Her family and her children support her at every stage. She is eligible for the old age pension but her name was not included. She told her concern about the old age pension and requested the worker to kindly facilitate her so that she receives her old age pension. The worker decided to help Devki in the process of receiving old age pension through the help of social work intervention.

Social Work Intervention

After comprehending the case in detail, the caseworker designed a set of intervention goals to address the pension problem of Devki. The goals include assisting the *Gram Prdhan* about the pension issue of Devki to facilitate the *Gram Prdhan* and Devki, to arrange the required documents for Devki. The worker had formulated strategic goals to address Devki's problem. The worker had applied specific strategies such as mediating between *Gram Prdhan* and Devki advocating the case of Devki and of course helping Devki. The worker's visits to Devki's home and *Gram Prdhan's* home on a number of times had built rapport and trust, which in turn helped the worker to make a successful intervention.

Methods and Techniques Applied

The worker had applied various methods and techniques while introducing social work intervention. Social Casework method was completely applicable in this case and the worker without any fail followed that. Home visits and advocacy helped the worker to obtain more information. He could get clarity on the issue and initiate the interaction with the client. The worker conducted several sessions with the *Gram Pradhan* and the client.

Values Followed

The worker had followed various values of social work such as dignity and worth of the person, importance of human relationship, integrity, service, competency, commitment, and responsibility. Dignity and worth of the persons involved in the case was evident throughout the intervention process. Worker showed respect for every relationship, which he made during the process of casework and always proved his integrity. The worker had taken the case wholeheartedly to help Devki as a professional social work practitioner, which is his 'value of service'. The worker had tactfully solved all the complicated problems with his skills and capacities, which proved his competence. The worker's professional commitment and responsibility were seen throughout the process of the case. The value of responsibility was clearly evident in this casework as the worker could take up the entire casework process in several months.

Application of Social Work Principles

The worker had carefully planned several strategies for intervention as well as applied various principles of social casework such as the principle of acceptance, client's right to self-determination, communication, individualization and confidentiality, etc. The application of the principle of acceptance was evident in the worker's approach as he had accepted the situation and difficulties of Devki and understood her strengths, limitations, potentialities, weaknesses, and misunderstanding. The worker applied the principle of confidentiality in this case. This of course ensured professional commitment. The principle of communication had played crucial role in this case as the worker could transmit the information according to the situation. In this case, the worker had to apply the principle of controlled emotional involvement several times during the initial interaction with Devki. The principle of non-judgmental attitude played a crucial role, the worker never judged the client's approaches and choices.

Evaluation

By applying various methods and following certain principles, the worker could address the problems in this case with his extraordinary skills and humanity qualities apart from following the principles, values of social work at every step. Devki has started receiving her old age pension and therefore, she is very happy. Thus, the social work intervention could help in providing the right help in response to the needs of clients. The modest financial help in the form of old age pension helped in bringing happiness at the cross road of Devki's life.

Case of Mukesh

Personal Background

Mukesh, a 74-year-old man was born in an upper caste *Hindu* family. He resides in the *Madwana* village with his servant. The entire family of Mukesh lives in the Lucknow city and often visits him. He gained his formal education up to seventh standard but has adequate economic support. Mukesh's house is *pucca* (cemented) and furnished with all necessary provisions. He is physically healthy.

Problem Assessed

The worker studied the case thoroughly by doing home visits and conducted several sessions for the identifying his existing problems. Problem assessment is a systematic study of the client's circumstances where worker tried to secure each and every minute detail all and every fact about Mukesh that revealed his personality and the situation for appropriate intervention. After rigorous community visits, the worker established a strong rapport with Mukesh. Eventually after subsequent visits and detailed discussions with Mukesh, the worker understood his actual problems. Mukesh was suffering from a number of problems such as loneliness, sleeplessness, sadness, etc. Although, Mukesh has no social and financial problems but being alone at his residence in the village are the key causes of his problems. The worker decided to help Mukesh from these existing problems by using social work methods, techniques, principles, and values. The assessment phases gave realistic basis about Mukesh's social context.

Social Work Intervention

The objective of social work intervention is to alleviate Mukesh's distress while restoring, maintaining or enhancing the social functioning of his everyday life. After understanding the case in detail, the caseworker designed a set of intervention goals to address the problems of Mukesh. The worker had formulated strategic goals to address Mukesh's problem. The worker had applied specific strategies including conducting a number of sessions with Mukesh in order to retrieve more details about him in a professional way to resolve these issues. The worker took various sessions with Mukesh and tried to develop a coping mechanism so that Mukesh is able to solve his problems. The worker tried to convince Mukesh to live happily and suggested to do meditation and spiritual activities. The worker also met Mukesh's family and children and convinced them to visit his father alternatively along with the grandchildren at least on Sundays. The worker conducted various sessions with the family of Mukesh. Several visits to Mukesh's home helped the process of social work intervention.

Methods and Techniques Applied

Diverse methods and techniques were used in the process of social work intervention. Social Casework method was completely applicable in this case and the worker without any fail followed that. Home visits helped the worker to obtain detailed information. He could get clarity on the issue and initiate the interaction with Mukesh. The worker also conducted several interviews with Mukesh and his family members. To encourage the strength of Mukesh strength based practice method was administered as well. The worker provided inclusive counseling to Mukesh.

Values Followed

The worker had followed various social work values while dealing with Mukesh. Major core values of social work, which were evident in the case of Mukesh include competency, service, dignity and worth of the person, integrity, importance of human relationship, commitment, and responsibility. Dignity and worth of the persons involved in the case of Mukesh was evident throughout the intervention process. By using the value of competence, the worker had tactfully solved the complicated problems with his skills and capacities; the worker's professional commitment and responsibility were seen throughout the process while dealing with the case of Mukesh. The worker had taken the case sincerely to help Mukesh as a professional social work practitioner and applied the value of service. The value of integrity was evident in this casework as the worker could take up the entire casework process without negotiating Mukesh's integrity. The worker maintained human relationship with every person during the entire casework process.

Application of Social Work Principles

The worker had meticulously planned several strategies for intervention as well as applying various principles of social casework such as the principle of acceptance, confidentiality, individualization, evaluation, communication, client's right to self-determination, etc. Like all other previous clients, the principle of confidentiality was also followed in the case of Mukesh, which obviously ensured the professional commitment of the worker. The principle of communication had played a central role in this case as the worker could transmit the information according to the situation. The application of the principle of acceptance was evident in the worker's approach as he had accepted the situation and difficulties of Mukesh and understood his strengths, limitations, potentialities, weaknesses, and misunderstanding. The principle of controlled emotional involvement, which was applied, was really needed in social work interventions particularly with individuals. The principle of non-judgmental attitude played a crucial role, the worker never judged the client's approaches and choices. In this case, the worker had to apply the principle of controlled emotional involvement several times especially during the initial interaction with Mukesh.

Evaluation

The worker could address the problems in case of Mukesh by applying various methods and techniques and following certain values and principles. Of course, the worker used his skills and humanity qualities alongside following the principles, values of social work at every step. Post intervention reveals that Mukesh's family members visit every Sundays with their children. He is now happy to see his grandchildren. The meditational and spiritual activities have reduced his mental stress at some extent. Mukesh reported that at the moment he does not feel lonely or isolated. Mukesh further revealed that he is now in regular touch with his children and whenever anything is required, he is provided with. In this way, the social work intervention could improve the quality of life of Mukesh.

Case of Usha

Personal Background

Usha a 63-year-old widow resides in a nuclear family with her two sons in the *Madwana* village. Like Ramasare, this client (Usha) too belongs to OBC. She studied only till the third standard. Her husband died nine years ago. Her elder son was married but her younger son is yet to marry. She has access to basic facilities such as drinking water and toilet in her own house. Her house is semi *pucca* (half cemented). However, Usha does not have any source of income. Her elder son is an agriculture labourer and younger son is employed in the unorganized sector. She is dependent on her sons.

Problem Assessed

After establishing a strong rapport with Usha the worker studied the case thoroughly by doing home visits and conducted several sessions in order to her existing problems. In the process of problem assessment, the worker tried to secure in-depth details about Usha that revealed her personality and the situation for appropriate intervention. It was the initial phase in which the worker gained his first understanding about the need of his client. After several visits and detailed discussions with Usha, the worker understood the actual problems. Since Usha lost her husband nine years ago and both of her sons were unmarried at the time of her husband's demise, she was compelled to face many liabilities. Somehow, Usha could manage to get her elder son married. Usha reported that she faced enormous sufferings in her life—her husband was an agricultural labour and they lived in poverty. As a result, she faced serious economic hurdle to meet the daily living expenses of her family. Her children were not working at that time. Her husband's kith and kin who reside nearby seldom visit her and never showed love and affection towards her, nor did they supported her economically. Only after her children started working, she became economically better. Everything was going well but suddenly her daughter-in-law committed suicide. The parents of her daughter-in-law lodged a case against the entire family including Usha and all of them were jailed for a period of six months. Usha reported that there was some sort of misunderstanding between her elder son and her daughter-in-law. This misunderstanding led her daughter-in-law to commit suicide. Usha expressed regret and disappointment that she could not do anything. Her elder son supports her economically but he does not take any opinion or suggestion from his mother. Usha goes on to record that the misunderstanding between her son and her daughter-in-law was on a trivial matter, similar to issues of many families, which generally take place between a husband and a wife and can be resolved through a discussion between them. Usha laments that the incorrect decision of her daughter-in-law to end her life has maligned the name of disrepute to her family. Usha further bemoans that in the last phase of her life the humiliation she had been facing through her life in jail was mentally disturbing. This incident has resulted in a number of mental problems in Usha such as stress, depression, sleeplessness, loneliness, and anxiety, etc. Due to these problems, she has been suffering physically too falls sick frequently. The worker decided to help the client from her existing problems through the help of social work intervention.

Social Work Intervention

After assessing the case in detail, the caseworker designed a set of intervention goals to address the problem. The goals include motivating Usha through counseling and providing encouragement by identifying her strengths and ability. The worker had formulated strategic goals to address the client's problem. He applied specific strategies such as counselling, sensitisation and motivational programmes including conducting a number of sessions to obtain more details about the case in a professional way so that the problems of Usha can be resolved. The worker took several sessions with Usha over a period of six months and frequently visited her home to build a rapport and trust on them, which in turn helped the worker to make a successful intervention.

Methods and Techniques Applied

Social Casework method was completely applicable in this case and the worker without any fail followed that. Home visits helped the worker to obtain more information. He could get clarity on the issue and initiate the interaction with Usha. The worker also conducted several interviews with Usha, her children and other family members. To encourage the strength of her strength based practice method was administered as well.

Values Followed

Primary core values of social work, which were evident in the case of Usha include dignity and worth of the person, competency, commitment, integrity, and service. The worker had taken the case wholeheartedly to help the Usha as a professional social work practitioner. The worker showed the value of service while dealing with Usha. Dignity and worth of the persons involved in the case was evident throughout the intervention process. The worker had tactfully solved the complicated problem with his skills and capacities. The worker's professional commitment was seen throughout the process of the case. The value of integrity was clearly evident in this casework as the worker could take up the entire casework process in several months and showed respect for every relationship he made during the process of casework and always proved his integrity.

Application of Social Work Principles

The worker had designed several strategies for intervention as well as applying various principles of social casework such as the principle of acceptance, the client's right to self-determination, communication, individualization, and confidentiality, etc. The application of the principle of acceptance was evident in the worker's approach as he had accepted the situation and difficulties of the Usha and understood her strengths, limitations, potentialities, weaknesses, and misunderstanding. The worker applied the principle of confidentiality to ensure professional commitment. The principle of controlled emotional involvement that was applied by the worker was really needed in social work interventions particularly with individuals. In this case, the worker had to apply the principle of controlled emotional involvement several times during the initial interaction with Usha. The principle of non-judgmental attitude played a crucial role, the worker never judged the Usha's approaches and choices.

Evaluation

It was a difficult case in terms of nature of problem, associated with Usha. The worker had dealt with the case by applying suitable strategies in every context. By applying various methods, following certain principles, the worker could address the multiple problems in this case of Usha, of course with his extraordinary skills and humanity qualities apart from following the principles, values of social work at every step. Currently, the client started involving herself in daily routine works. She took up some embroidery work, which was facilitated by the worker with the help of an NGO. She is engaged in the work and as a result, her level of stress has gone down as compared to her pre intervention condition. She now takes normal sleep as well as feels less depressed. Her younger son looks after her now and provides every support. Her elder son, who was also disturbed by the incident, has started talking and sharing his feelings and emotions with his mother and brother. All these post intervention positive outcomes have brought some sense of relief and mental peace to Usha's lives but she keeps on thinking about her children's marriage.

GLOBAL OBSERVATION

All the six cases were unique in its nature with having varied problems. Social Work Intervention was very effective in improving the condition of the elderly. It is found that in few cases some issues were not resolved completely due to the limitations of the worker. In the case of Chaurana the eldest son was still behaving badly, but same time in the case of Ashok and Devki, the problems were almost fully resolved by the worker. Mukesh is happy as his family members are visiting regularly. Overall, all the case were successfully dealt by the worker. Therefore, social work intervention is highly relevant in the care of aged to improve their quality of life.

6

Working with Elderly

Old age is the last stage of one's life and it is one of the most difficult stages of life both physically and mentally. This is mainly due to the general decline of health and chronic illness. This stage becomes more difficult because of increasing financial dependence, lack of opportunities and inabilities to gain social contacts, and the pains of isolation and bereavement due to the death of the loved ones, especially life partners, family members and friends. Indian society is also witnessing rapid changes in the family system. This research unfolded that changes in the family system has further added to the challenges caused by physical and mental health problems confronted frequently during the old age. Joint families and extended family system are slowly disappearing. Shifts in the pattern of life and roles have affected the elderly people, which can be ignored by no one—the society, the governments or the social scientists. The changing values of the family system along with the lack of adequate government support have increasingly contributed to the growing dissatisfaction among the older generation. The research findings suggest that for various nuanced reasons (such as families living in other cities; loneliness, worries about children, dispute within the family, poverty, etc.), the family members fail to offer the desired level of care to their elderly. The values of the Indian society used to bestow tremendous respect to the elderly. Central status was given to the elderly at home in all matters, whether it is related to food, leisure, financial matters and any household decisions. Since due to advancement in medical sciences the mortality rate of the aged has gone down drastically and the changes that are occurring in the treatment of the aged, both within families and outside, have led to longer life of the elderly, thereby, the new problems that has emerged, challenges the adjustment ability of the elderly in different areas of life. Individuals, families, society and governments alone cannot meet these new emergent problems. Rather, it should become a priority concern for all, especially for social scientists, social workers, psychologists, counselors and gerontologists.

FINDINGS

The finding of the study revealed that social work intervention plays a significant role in the care of the aged. Segment wise relative findings during pre and post-intervention of the elderly have been presented below which examines the importance of social work intervention in the area of elderly care.

Basic Necessities

Drinking Water Facility

Pre and post data analysis revealed that before intervention, majority of the respondents were dependent on government hand pumps; whereas the dependency on government hand pumps, has been reduced after social work intervention in *Madwana.* Data showed that currently 48 per cent of the respondents have their own hand pumps, which show the impact of interventions on 13 per cent of the elderly in *Madwana.* Post-intervention assessment found that one respondent in *Goila* had installed his own hand pump with his own resources.

Toilet Facility

Pre-intervention assessment revealed that majority of the respondents had no accessibility to toilets in their own houses. Data showed that after intervention about 18 per cent of the respondents were motivated to construct toilets at their houses with the support of their family members in *Madwana* which results a significant impact of social work intervention as compared to control village where no improvement have been recorded with respect to toilet facility during the post-intervention assessment.

Government Pension

In spite of the eligibility for receiving old age and widow pension, majority of the respondents could not avail the benefit of government pension scheme. Post-intervention data unveiled that about 8 per cent of the respondents were benefited by social work intervention for receiving the old age (5%) and widow (2.5%) pension in *Madwana* whereas no changes were found in *Goila.*

The food for the respondents is still arranged by their spouses, daughter-in-law's and relatives in both the villages but the condition of the elderly who were alone has been improved in *Madwana* as compared to *Goila* as some of the respondents are being provided food by the family members. The respondents from both the villages spend their leisure time mostly with spouses, family members, relatives, friends, neighbours and children. There are no major changes in both the villages with regard to their leisure time.

Physical and Mental Health

Eye Sight

The elderly were suffering from vision problem in both the villages. The specific reasons for low vision were not told by the respondents but few of them were found to be suffering from cataract. The eye sight of approximately 53 per cent of the respondents was not good during pre-intervention assessment in *Madwana.* Post-intervention data revealed that after social work intervention 20 per cent of the respondents have been benefited. Two new cases of low vision were found during post-intervention assessment in *Goila*.

Hearing Capacity

Pre-intervention assessment found that the hearing capacity of approximately 43 per cent in *Goila* and 50 per cent in *Madwana* was not good. Post-intervention assessment showed that the hearing capacity of around 8 per cent of the respondents have been improved after social work intervention in *Madwana* with the support of hearing aids. Post-intervention data showed that about 5 per cent of the respondents were increased whose hearing capacity was not good in *Goila*.

Problem in Physical Movement

The pre-intervention study found that more than half of the respondents were experiencing problem in their physical movement to a large extent. Post-intervention assessment data revealed that after social work intervention, the physical movement of approximately 5 per cent of the respondents has been improved in *Madwana* whereas without intervention 3 per cent improvement was found in *Goila*.

Frequency of Falling Ill

The pre-intervention assessment showed that about 38 per cent of the respondents in *Goila* and 40 per cent in *Madwana* fall sick more than 4 times in a year. Post-intervention assessment data revealed that after social work intervention, the frequency of falling ill more than 4 times in a year was reduced in the *Madwana* up to 10 per cent whereas 3 per cent improvement was found in *Goila*. The significant impact of social work intervention has been examined in the frequency of falling ill.

Effect of Physical Health on Activities of Daily Living

In the pre-intervention study, it was found that physical health problem affects about 48 per cent of the elderly in *Goila* and 40 per cent in *Madwana* in their activities of daily living (ADL). Post-intervention assessment found that after social work intervention the effect of physical health reduced to a large extent on 23 per cent of the respondents in *Madwana*. Improved physical health helped these respondents to carry on their daily activities in a better way. The effect of physical health to large extent on ADL has been increased on approximately 3 per cent of the respondents during post-intervention study in *Goila*.

Ability to Express the Emotions

In pre-intervention assessment, about 45 per cent of the respondents in *Goila* and 55 per cent in *Madwana* were hardly able to express their emotions with their family members. Post-intervention data revealed that social work intervention has improved the ability to express the emotions of 10 per cent elderly in *Madwana* whereas in Goila, the ability to express emotions of the elderly failed to improve. Surprisingly and yet sadly, the research revealed that approximately 3 per cent more of the elderly in Goila fails to express their emotions with their family members.

Depression

Pre-intervention assessment found that more than half of the respondents were experiencing depression to a large extent in *Madwana* whereas post-intervention assessment revealed that the depression to a large extent has been reduced after social work intervention and about 15 per cent of the respondents have been benefited from the intervention. Post-intervention data showed the improvement in depression to a large extent on about 5 per cent of the respondents in *Goila*.

Fear of Death

Pre-intervention data showed that about 45 per cent of the respondents in *Goila* and 48 per cent in *Madwana* had suffered from the fear about death to a large extent. Post-intervention assessment found that after social work intervention the fear of death has reduced in approximately 15 per cent of the respondents in *Madwana*. Post-intervention data also revealed that the fear of death has increased to a large extent in approximately 13 per cent of the respondents in *Goila*.

Sleeplessness

Pre-intervention study found that about 48 per cent of the respondents in *Goila* and 40 per cent in *Madwana* experience sleeplessness. Post-intervention assessment found that after social work intervention the problem of sleeplessness has reduced in 10 per cent of the respondents in *Madwana* to a large extent. Post-intervention data also revealed that the problem of sleeplessness has increased in approximately 8 per cent of the respondents in *Goila* to a large extent.

Loneliness

In the pre-intervention present study, it was found that about 38 per cent of the respondents in *Goila* and 30 per cent in *Madwana* experienced loneliness to a great extent. However, post-intervention assessment found that the problem of loneliness been reduced in approximately 13 per cent of the respondents in *Madwana*. Post-intervention data further revealed that the problem of loneliness has increased to a large extent in 10 per cent of the respondents in *Goila*.

Forgetfulness

Pre-intervention study found that about 38 per cent of the respondents in both Goila and Madwana were experiencing forgetfulness. Post-intervention assessment found that as a result of social work intervention, the problem of forgetfulness has reduced in 5 per cent of the respondents in *Madwana*. Post-intervention data further revealed that the problem of forgetfulness to has increased in 5 per cent of the respondents in *Goila*.

Effect of Loss of Dear Ones

Pre-intervention study found that loss of dear ones affect more than half of the respondents to a large extent in both the villages. Post-intervention assessment found that after social work intervention the effect of loss of dear ones has been reduced in 20 per cent of the respondents in *Madwana*. Post-intervention data also revealed that the effect of loss of dear ones has increased in approximately 13 per cent of the respondents in *Goila*.

Support System, Elder Abuse and Neglect

Family Support

Pre-intervention study found that about 48 per cent of the respondents in the *Goila* and *Madwana* were not receiving good family support. Post-intervention assessment found that after social work intervention about 25 per cent of the respondents have been benefited with good family support in *Madwana*. Post-intervention data also revealed that about 5 per cent of the respondents in *Goila* do not receive good family support.

Social Support

Pre-intervention assessment showed that around 50 per cent of the respondents in the *Goila* and *Madwana* were not receiving good social support. Post-intervention assessment found that after social work intervention about 13 per cent of the respondents received benefits from good social support in *Madwana*. Post-intervention data revealed that about 8per cent of the respondents in *Goila* fail to receive social support.

Government Support

Pre-intervention study revealed that about 95 per cent of the respondents in *Goila* and 90 per cent in *Madwana* hardly receive any government support. After post-intervention assessment it was found that approximately 15 per cent of the respondents started receiving government support in *Madwana*, however, the research also unfolded that no respondent in *Goila* received any benefit from the government.

Elder Abuse

Pre-intervention study showed that about 48 per cent of the respondents in the *Goila* and 50 per cent in *Madwana* experienced elder abuse to a large extent in their daily lives. Post-intervention assessment found that elder abuse reduced to a large extent in approximately 18 per cent of the respondents in *Madwana*. This obviously is a significant impact of social work intervention. Post-intervention data further revealed that in Goila, the elder abuse reduced to a large extent in around 8 per cent of the respondents.

Neglect

Pre-intervention data revealed that about 45 per cent of the respondents in *Goila* and 58 per cent in *Madwana* experienced neglect to a large extent in their life. Post-intervention assessment found that after social work intervention neglect of older people decreased to a great extent in 20 per cent of the respondents in *Madwana*. This indicates a positive impact of social work intervention. In addition, post-intervention data also revealed that neglect of older people reduced largely in 5 per cent of the respondents in *Goila*.

RECOMMENDATIONS

India has been described as a 'young-nation' where majority live in the rural area. However, with declining birth rates and longer life expectancies, elderly population is rapidly increasing. A shift in the society has been observed in the institutional care of the elderly in rural area. Although central and state governments have initiated several schemes to provide better health services, and economic support through various ministries and departments, yet the full benefits of such schemes fail to reach the rural elderly. Elders are the backbone of the society as they can guide the young generation in nation building. It is the duty of every citizen of India to provide all necessary care and support to maintain the dignity and worth of the elderly. The present study has brought about some findings pertaining to their care. Based on the findings some recommendations are made for the care and protection of the rural elderly in India.

Community Sensitisation Programmes

There is an urgent need to sensitize the rural community for the well-being of the elderly. The research reveals that elders are not much cared for by the community and therefore, community members must be sensitized for elder care. Some of the initiatives could include:

- To sensitize rural community, community sensitisation programmes must be launched with the support of local bodies and community members.
- Youth clubs can be formed to help and support the elders facing difficulties in their daily life.
- Non-governmental organisations (NGOs) must step forward to take up sensitisation programmes to enable the rural aged for enhancing their social skills for better adjustment.

Revisiting Family Values

- There is an urgent need to revisit the family values in the context of the present social scenario.
- The family values such as love, care, protection, respect, dignity, coherence, compassion must be imparted to the young generation.
- The importance of elderly in our society must be highlighted among the youths and adults.
- Teaching children about societal values through school curriculum could be one of the ways of helping young generation to imbibe social and family values.

Use of Media

- Media can play a vital role in sensitising and making awareness among the people about the issues related to the elderly. It can highlight the best positive practices prevailing in the society as a tool to sensitization and awareness building. Small efforts pertaining to elder care need to be recognized.
- All India Radio (AIR) community radios can disseminate information by broadcasting programmes pertaining to elder care and their importance in the family as well in the society as it has good reach in all parts of India especially in the rural sector.
- Television (TV) is another medium for making awareness in the society for the care and protection of the elderly.
- Periodicals especially on elder issues and concerns would be an affective medium to transmit the information about the elder care and protection in the society.
- Community Radio would be very effective at local level for highlighting the local issues of the society including elder care and family support.
- Folk Media would be another extraordinary medium to raise

the issues of elders by using local cultural method for disseminating information.

- Nukkad Natak, Folkways, Awareness Campaign, Posters, Screening of Documentaries etc.

Involvement of Schools of Social Work

- Involvement of Schools of Social Work for well-being of the elderly in various forms would be an effective way to help the helpless.
- Rural Camps can be organised on the theme of elder care.
- Through internships, students can be placed in the community or institutions where they can work on elderly issues and problems.
- Practicum is the important aspect of social work education and students are supposed to be equipped with various skills and methods. In social work practicum, working with the elderly component can be included so that students can practice social work skills and methods among the elderly for their betterment.
- Placing students in the community or institutions for the elderly care through Block Placement would be another step to help the elders by involving social work professionals.

Involvement of National Service Scheme (NSS)

- The volunteers of National Service Schemes can be placed for their field work in the community or institutions for making awareness about the elder care and their importance in the society. Interventions also can be done through NSS volunteers for the issues pertaining to the elderly.

Employing Social Work Professionals

- Professional social workers are equipped with skills and

knowledge to deal with social problems. They understand the human dynamics and behaviours of an individual. Employing social work professionals in rural areas by government, NGOs as well as Faith Based Organizations would be one-step to provide help and care to the needy persons specially the aged.

- This research has shown that the rural elderly are not able to avail the facilities of the government schemes and programmes, therefore, professional social workers will be able to help them in their rights. Therefore, social work professionals need to fill in the gap with regard to mental health where our rural socio-cultural milieu is not sensitive enough to deal with such problems.
- There is also a need for integrated approach to provide legal, health, social services and other allied services for the elderly, which only professionally qualified social worker can provide.
- Social environment plays a crucial role in one's life. Professionally qualified social workers have the skills to understand the social environment of an individual. In the context of the elder care, social work professionals can help the elderly in adjusting in their social environment, which affects their well-being.

Involvement of Panchayati Raj Institutions

- Panchayati Raj Institution (PRI) can play a vital role in enhancing and ensuring the well-being of the elderly. In fact, it is an implementing agency in rural areas for both central and state governments, which can ensure maximum benefits of the government schemes and programmes related to old age. As this research reflects that, the health condition of the elderly in rural area is not good. Therefore, regular health camps for the rural elderly can be organised by the PRI in collaboration with the social work professionals.

Promotion of Research on the Care of Rural Aged

- There is a need for more research on the issues of the elderly. Experimental research on the elderly must be promoted and the institutions of social work must provide adequate scholarships and grants for more research on the elderly. Community based interventions must be promoted in the area of research.
- There is also a need for policy amendments to include mandatory social work/counselling interventions. Code of Ethics for Social Work Intervention must be developed and adopted by the social work professionals while working with the elderly.

Bibliography

Ananthanaraman, R.N. (1982). The Psychological Aspects of India. In Desai, K.G. (Ed.), *Aging In India*. Bombay: Tata Institute of Social Sciences.

Anderson, S.A., Candyce, S.R., and Walter, R.S. (1983). *Perceived Marital Quality and Family Life Cycle Categories: A Further Analysis*. Journal of Marriage and the Family 45, pp. 127-139.

Antonucci, T. (1990). Personal Characteristics, Social Support and Social Behaviour. In Binstock, R. and George, L. (Eds.), *Handbook of Ageing and the Social Sciences (3rd edition)*. USA.: Academic Press. pp. 205-216.

Atal, Y. (2001). The United Nations and Ageing. *Indian Journal of Gerontology*, 15 (1 and 2), pp. 1-9.

Bagchi, K. (Ed.). (1997). *Elderly Females in India—their Status and Suffering*, New Delhi: Society for Gerontological Research and Helpage India.

Bagga, A. and Sakurakar, A. (1999). Twilight Years and Health of Older Women. *Indian Journal of Gerontology*, 14 (3 and 4), pp. 114-124.

Bali, A.P. (1996). Role of Family in the Care of the Elderly: Changing Care Giving Situation. In Kumar, V. (Ed.), *Aging: Indian Perspective and Global Scenario*. New Delhi: All India Institute of Medical Sciences.

Bali, A.P. (1997). Invoking Local Initiatives in Health Care Education of the Elderly in Rural Areas. *Research and Development Journal*, 3(3).

Bali, A.P. (2001). *Care of the Elderly in India: Changing Configurations*. Shimla: Indian Institute of Advanced Study.

Bartlett, H.M. (1970). *The Common Base of Social Work Practice*. New York: NASW.

Bayer, G.H., and Woods, M.E. (1963). *Living and Activity Patterns of the Aged*. Research Report No. 6. New York: Centre for Housing and Environmental Studies, Comell University.

Beck, A. Resnik, H., and Lettieri, D. (1974). The Prediction of Suicide. In *Encyclopedia of Social Work*, (Volume 2, Edition 18). Silver Spring: National Association of Social Researchers.

Berkman, B. and Harootyan, L. (Eds.). (2003). *Social Work and Health Care in an Aging Society: Education, Policy, Practice, and Research*. New York: Springer Publishing Company, Inc.

Birren, J.E. (1964). *The Psychology of Aging*. Englewood Cliffs, New Jersey: Prentice Hall, Inc.

Birren, J.E., and Cunningham, W.R. (1985). Research on the Psychology of Aging. In Birren, J.E., and Sehaie, K.W. (Eds.), *Handbook of the Psychology of Aging (2nd edition)*. New York: Van Nostrand Reinhold.

Birren, J.E., and Renner, V.J. (1980). Concepts and Issues of Mental Health and Aging. In Birren, J.E., and R.B. Sloane (Eds.), *Handbook of Mental Health and Aging*. Englewood Cliffs, New Jersey: Prentice Hall, Inc.

Birren, J.E., and Renner, V.J. (1977). Research on the Psychology of Aging: Principles and Experimentation. In Birren, J.E., and Sehaie, K.W. (Eds.), *Handbook of the Psychology of Aging (2nd edition)*. New York: Van Nostrand Reinhold.

Birren, J.E., and Zarit, J.M. (1985). Concepts of Health, Behaviour, and Aging. In Birren, J.E., and Livingston, J. (Eds.), *Cognition, Stress and Aging*. Englewood Cliffs, New Jersey: Prentice Hall, Inc.

Biswas, S.K. (1987). *Aging in Contemporary India*. Calcutta: Indian Anthropological Society.

Blood, R.O., and Wolfe, D.W. (1960). *Husbands and Wives: The Dynamics of Married Living*. Glencoe, Illinois: Freepress.

Boehm, W. (1959). *Curriculum Study of the Council on Social Work Education*. Vol. I. New York: Publisher.

Bose, A. (2001). Demographic Transition', *Seminar,* 488, pp. 35-39.

Bose, A.B. and Gangrade, K.D. (1988). *Aging in India: Problems and Potentialities*. New Delhi: Abhinav Publications.

Bowling, A. Farqhar, M. and Browne, P. (1991). *Life Satisfaction and Associations with Social Network and Support Variables in Three Samples of Elderly People*. International Journal of Geriatric Psychiatry Vol. 6, pp. 549-566.

Busse, E.W. (1969). Theories of Aging. In Busse, E.W., and Pfeiffer, E. (Eds.), *Behaviour and Adaptation in Later Life*. Boston: Little Brown.

Busse, E.W., and Blazer, D.G. (1980). The Theories and Processes of Aging. In Busse, E.W., and Blazer, D.G. (Eds.), *Handbook of Geriatric Psychiatry*. New York: Litton Educational Publishing Inc.

Caplan, G. (1974). *Support Systems and Community Mental Health*. New York: Behavioural Publications.

Carstensen, L.L., and Lang, F.R., (1994). *Close Emotional Relationships in Late Life: Further Support for Practice Aging in the Social Domain*. Psychology and Aging Vol. 9(2), pp. 315-324.

Census of India, (1992). *Aging in India,* Occasional Paper no. 2, Office of the Registrar General and Census Commissioner, New Delhi.

Chakraborti, P. (1997). Who cares for the Elderly? A Study of Health Management and Care. In N.K. Chadha (ed.), *Aging and the Aged—Challenges before Indian Gerontology.* Vadodara: Friends Publications.

Chowdhry, D.P. (1992). *Aging and the Aged.* New Delhi: Inter India Publication.

Cobb, S. (1976). *Social Support as a Moderator of Life Stress.* Psychosomatic Medicine 38, pp. 300-314.

Comfort, A. (1964). *Aging: The Biology of Senescence.* New York: Harper and Row.

Coulshed, V. and Orme, J. (1998). *Social Work Practice: An Introduction* (Edition 3). London: Macmillan Press.

Dandekar, K. (1996). *The Elderly in India,* New Delhi: Sage.

Davis, K. (1949). *Human Society.* New York: Macmillan.

Feinson, M.C. (1986). *Aging Widows and Widowers: Are there Mental Health Differences?* International Journal of Aging and Human Development 23, pp. 241-255.

Field, D., Minkler, M. Falk, R.F., and Leino, E.V. (1993). *The Influence of Health on Family Contacts and Family Feelings in Advanced Old Age: A Longitudinal Study.* Journal of Gerontology, 48. pp. 18-28.

Fremouw, W., Perczel, M. and Ellis, T. (1990). *Suicide Risk Assessment and Response Guidelines.* New York: Pergamon Press.

Gangrade, K.D. (1988). Crisis of Values: A Sociological Study of the Old and the Young. In Bose, A.B. and Gangrade K.D. *The Ageing in India: Problems and Potentialities.* New Delhi: Abhinav.

Gangrade, K.D. (1989). Emerging Conception of Ageing in India: A Socio-cultural Perspective. *Eastern Anthropologist,* 42(2), pp. 151-69.

Gilford, R. (1984). *Contrasts in Marital Satisfaction throughout Old Age: An Exchange Theory Analysis.* Journal of Gerontology 39, pp. 325-333.

Golan, N. (1986). Crisis Theory. In F.J. Turner (Ed.), *Social Work Treatment: Interlocking Theoretical Approaches*—3rd Editions (pp. 303-317). New York: The Free Press.

Government of India. (2011). *Situational Analysis of the Elderly in India.* Central Statistic Office, Ministry of Statistics and Programme Implementation.

Gulati, L. and Rajan, I.S. (1999). The Added Years—Elderly in India and Kerala. *Economic and Political Weekly,* XXXIV (44), pp. WS41-46.

Hammen, C. (1995). The Social Context of Risk for Depression. In K. Craig and K.S. Dobson (Eds.), *Anxiety and Depression in Adults and Children.* Thousand Oaks: Sage Publications.

Handler, P. (1960). Radiation and Aging. In Shock, N.W. (Ed.), *Aging: Some Social and Biological Aspects.* Washington, D.C.: American Association for the Advancement of Science.

Havighurst, R.J. (1961). *Successful Aging.* Gerontologist 1, pp. 4-7.

Help Age India. (2008). *Right Based Advocacy for Disadvantaged Elders.* New Delhi: Programme Division Help Age India.

Hollis, F. (1972). *Casework: A Psychological Therapy,* (Edition 2), New York: Random House.

Hollis, F. and Woods, M. (1981). *Casework: A Psychological Therapy*, (Edition 3), New York: Random House.

Holosko, M.J. and Feit, M.D. (Eds.). (2004). *Social Work Practice with the Elderly.* Toronto: Canadian Scholars Press, Inc.

Hurlock, E.B. (1975). *Development Psychology.* New Delhi: Tata Mc Graw Hill.

Jai Prakash, I. (1987). Satisfaction with Social Supports and Mental Health: A Study of Age and Sex Difference. *Journal of Personality and Clinical Studies,* 3(2), pp; 131-34.

Jamuna, D., and Reddy, L.K. (1992). *Dynamics of In-Law Equations.* Aging and Society: The Indian Journal of Gerontology 111 (4), pp. 40-43.

Johnson, M.L. (Ed.). (2005). *The Cambridge Handbook of Age and Ageing.* New York: Cambridge University Press.

Kishore, S. (2001). Ageing Pains. *Seminar,* 488, pp. 30-34.

Kohli, A.S. (1996). *Social Situation of the Aged in India.* New Delhi: Anmol Publications.

Kumar Panda, P. (1998). *The Elderly in Rural Orissa: Alone in Distress.* Economic and Political Weekly, June 20, pp. 1545-1550.

Kumar, S.V. (1991). *Family life and socio-economic problems of the aged.* New Delhi: Ashish Publishing House.

Lal Das, D.K. (2010). Introduction to Methods of Research in Social Work. In Gracious Thomas (Eds.), *Social Work Research MSW 006.* New Delhi: IGNOU.

Lal Das, D.K. (2010). Introduction to Social Work Research. In Gracious Thomas (Eds.), *Social Work Research MSW 006.* New Delhi: IGNOU.

Lowy, L. (1955). *Adult Education and Group Work.* New York: Whiteside and William R. Morrow.

Lowy, L. (1974). *Function of Social Work in a Changing Society.* Boston: Milford House.

Lowy, L. (1979). *Social Work with the Aging.* New York: Harper & Row.

Malinwoski, B. (1958). *Crime and Custom in a Savage Society.* London: Routledge & Kegan Paul.

Maslow, A. (1954). *Motivation and Personality.* New York: Saunders.

McCall, G. and Simmons, J.L. (1966). *Identities and Interactions.* New York: The Free Press.

Myrdal, G. (1968). *At the 14th International Conference of Social Welfare.* Helsinki. Publisher.

NSSO. (1998). *The Aged in India, A Socio-Economic Profile,* 52nd Round (1995-96).

Palmore, E. and Clark, L. (1972). *Health and social factors related to life satisfaction.* Journal of Health and Social Behaviour 13: 68-80.

Panda, A.K. (2005). *Elderly Women in Megapolish.* New Delhi: Concept Publishing Company.

Parmeswaran, E. and Beena, C. (2002). *An Invitation to Psychology.* Hyderabad: Neelkamal Publications.

Parsons, T. (1951). *The Social System*. New York: Free Press.

Rastogi, H.S. (1964). Old Age Pensions in UP. *Social Welfare,* 10(11), pp. 24-27.

Ray, M. and Phillips, J. (2012). *Social Work With Older People*. London: Palgrave Macmillan.

Rockstein, M. (1974). Preface. In Rockstein, M., Sussman, M.L. and Chesky, J. (Eds.), *Theoretical Aspects of Aging*. New York: Academic Press.

Shaheen, A. (1994). *Old Age Among Slum Dweller*. New Delhi: South Asian Publications.

Shanas, E., Townsend, P., Wedderburn and Others (1968). *Old People in Three Industrial Societies*. London: Routledge and Kegan Paul.

Shock, N.W. (1977). Biological Theories of Aging. In Birren, J.E. and Schaie, K.W. (Eds.), *Handbook of the Psychology of Aging*. New York: Van Nonstrand Reinhold.

Siporin, M. (1974). *Introduction to Social Work Practice*. New York: Macmillan.

Soodan, K.S. (1975). *Aging in India*. Calcutta: Minerva Associates Publications Pvt. Ltd.

Sujaya, C.P. (1999). Some Comments on National Policy on Older Persons. *Economic and Political Weekly,* XXXIV (44), pp. WS72-74.

Tibbitts, C. (Ed.) (1960). *Handbook of Social Gerontology: Societal Aspects of Aging*. Chicago: University of Chicago Press.

UNFPA Report 2012. Retrieved on June 9, 2014, from http:// www.unfpa.org

UNO. (1995). *Implications of Asia's Population Future for Older People in the Family.* Oxford University Press.

Wall, R. (1989). The Living Arrangement of the Elderly in Europe in the 1980's. In Bytheway, B., Keil, T., and Others (Eds.), *Becoming and Being Old: Sociological Approaches to Later Life*. London: Sage Publications.

Ward, R.A. (1979). *The Aging Experience—An Introduction to Social Gerontology.* New York: J.B. Lippincott Company.

Warren, R.L. (1963). *The Community in America*. Skokie: Rand McNally.

Webster, P.S. and Herozog, A.R. (1995). *Effects of Parental Divorce and Memories of Family Problems on Relationships between Adult Children and their Parents. Journal of Gerontology 50 B, pp. 24-34.*

Weiss, P. (1966). Aging: A Corollary Development. In Shock, N.W. (Ed.), *Perspectives in Experimental Gerontology*. Springfield, Illinois: Charles C Thomas.

Weiss, R. (1973). *Loneliness: the experience of emotional and social isolation*. Cambridge, Mass: MIT Press.

Weiss, R.S. (1974). *Loneliness: The Experience of Emotional and Social Isolation.* Cambridge. MA: MIT Press.

Wenger, G.C. (1984). *The Supportive Network, Coping with Old Age*. National Institute of Social Services Library 46, London.

Index